Parenting
Scholar Athletes

*Four Keys to Raising
Responsible and
Independent Children*

PILAR KELLENBARGER

*Michelle,
Keep on hiking! :)

Pilar K*

To my daughters who taught me everything I know.

Copyright © 2021 by Pilar Kellenbarger

All rights reserved. No part of this publication may be reproduced, distributed, or transmitted in any form or by any means, including photocopying, recording,or other electronic or mechanical methods, without the prior written permission of the publisher, except in the case of brief quotations embodied in critical reviews and certain other noncommercial uses permitted by copyright law. For permission requests, please write to: pilar.regan@gmail.com

ISBN: 978-0-578-90949-3

Cover design: Markell Design

Text design: Andy at meadencreative.com

Contents

Introduction

The Dream of Becoming a Scholar Athlete

As parents, we all hear the stories of those amazing athletes in college who stepped up in their sport and received scholarships for their efforts. We're wondering what goes into that journey. What does a day in the life of that look like? Some of us are wondering how much it'll cost as well as what different aspects they have to overcome to get to that spot. It seems like out of the blue, these astonishing athletes are moving from high school to college playing for NCAA. In reality, they started as a young child shooting hoops in their driveway, kicking endless soccer balls into a net rain or shine, swimming countless miles, or serving endless volleyballs in a humid and hot warehouse at 95 degrees. As our little athlete grows, we want to help them join that group of being a scholar athlete.

We want to help our child with their dreams of being a scholar athlete. While we watch them play their sport and observe their grades and study habits, we see that they have some aspects of what it takes to be a scholar athlete. Since it's an avenue you know little about, here's a book to help point you in the right direction and help you keep your promise to help them achieve their dream.

Becoming a coachable scholar athlete, it all starts with a dream, but must be combined with the right tools to help the dreamer make it to their finish line. These little angels must be given the right amount of love, nutrition, and guidance to make it to their goal. These are just some aspects that are involved in the four keys I used which are Love, Communication, Consistency, and Schedule. Within these four keys, there are many other areas that must be discussed and planned in order for your child to bloom into the scholar athlete of their dream.

Why I Wrote This Book

I was blessed with two daughters two and a half years apart and was blessed with being a stay at home mom for their beginning years. As they grew, I saw how they were very interested in their studies and their sport. They both started as surf girls and continued their independent style into swimming. While on the local YMCA swim team, they both rose as top seated in their events. Once in middle school, they both fell in love with volleyball. It turned out that one went back to swimming in high school level and joined water polo while the other grew to almost six foot and continued on the volleyball circuit. If I look back at their journey to becoming scholar athletes, I had the know-how and they had the brains.

Friends were the ones who insisted that I put down in writing how I raised my children. They reminded me that there are many parents who would need the help. They've seen my daughters' accomplishments and knew it was the way in which I raised them. By sticking to the simple qualities of the 70's, all I had to do was add my four keys that helped keep me somewhat sane through it all and my girls moving forward.

My Passion to Help Other Parents

Now, don't get me wrong, these children didn't become the scholar athletes with stress free, easy- peazy days. We had our weeks of no television because of failure to follow rules. There were the stressful days when youngsters cried because they wanted their way and were going to do anything they could to obtain it.

I feel there is a real void of knowledge out there on raising children. With busy days for most, parents are looking for answers, successful ideas, and concepts that work. My hope is to help others by sharing my experiences and thoughts from my journey with my girls through to their college years, give real world concepts of children and their upsets and what it is really going to look like, and offer keys to becoming wise parents with healthy and successful children.

The Four Keys to Raising Strong Children

The four keys to raising strong children successfully are Love, Schedule, Communication, and Consistency. These are the four keys to stick to when raising outstanding creatures if you want them to emulate angels. There are many skills involved inside each key. As you follow these, more ideas will fill your mind and heart.

Key: Love

I believe *Love* is the first and foremost noun and verb that is present on a daily basis in our children's lives. It will come into play on the happiest and most frustrating days. Keep it close to your heart and alongside your brain, since it will help you during your most struggling times. Let it always be present as they reach for their dream of being a scholar athlete.

If we really think about it, children are here because of love. They are here because our love was put into the universe and they were sent as our answer. They come to us as angels toting their life lessons for us to learn, too. Whether you believe or not that there is a higher Source, these little creatures will change your thinking toward that source and likewise show and teach you the lessons left for you to learn while on this scholar athlete journey.

Key: Schedule

Schedule was my best friend. It kept me on time for every business meeting and important engagement. Once I became a mom at home, I knew I needed to implement this concept into my daily hectic life. Take your most important morals and values and make them number one in your family's life. The author of *7 Habits of Highly Effective People*, Stephen Covey once said, "The key is not to prioritize what's on your schedule, but to schedule your priorities." I ran each day with my children similar to one of a pre-school. I wanted my children to experience some form of learning each day.

I feel when you create a day using balance and schedule; it becomes a habit for your children's lives. They look for something to learn every day. Scheduling your priorities and teaching this to your children at a young age will help your children create successful non stressful lives of their own to prepare them for the stress that comes along with being a scholar athlete.

Remember, what you expose to your children is learned. I scheduled learning as a daily aspect of their life which in turn is what they learned to do during their years in school. If you teach them how to schedule and what to schedule, they begin to use this in their own lives as they grow from elementary years, through middle school, and into high school. Our youngsters need to practice this in their lives of juggling school work, sports, friendships, and hobbies. Once learned, you can rest assure they will put it to practice during college.

Key: Communication

Communication is a must. For those parents that begin to feel moist palms, it is not anything to fear. I will help you find the best words for any circumstance. Keeping the window of communication open is only going to aid in the success of your child. By bringing this into the everyday life of your children, it will help those parents who feel they do not have good skills in this area. As they say, practice makes perfect. Communication has to be practiced before they enter even middle school and/or high school. When communication is available, your future scholar athlete will become accountable for their actions.

My children grew up in the late 90's and 2000's, during the huge burst of technology era with the cell phone. Technology started as phones with texting capability and the fun of games. Because children saw their parents with them, they wanted them. I wouldn't let mine touch it. I treated it as if it were a cigarette. Would we let our baby or toddler hold and touch a cigarette? Absolutely not! Children will only fight for what is given. This book will help parents take charge of technology in a loving manner by practicing communication skills. Here is where consistency and communication will come together.

Key: Consistency

Consistency is the steadfast adherence to the same principle or course you may take. It is also the harmonious agreement of holding something firm and steady to retain something. This key will keep you sane if you use it and not falter. Consistency must be present in your rules, rewards, consequences, and outcomes you construct if you want your children to be independent people. Because it is ever present in the adult world, letting your children experience it early on a daily basis is imperative. My experiences will help show you the way.

What This Book Will Do For You

As your child becomes older, technology is ever present in the home as well as in school. This book helps us remember who is boss. This book will model how to be consistent with your rules, use rewards and consequences, and teach them the proper use of the devices. I'll show you how to tackle that beast.

Almost gone are the days of sitting around the kitchen table and living room telling our family stories. If taught in the correct manner, you will find your own children giving you the reminder of no phones at the dinner table. My girls love reminding us at home or at the restaurant table. Because they learned consistency, they practiced it. This book helps parents understand the impact technology has on their brain and gives strategies to keep our children aware of their choices when it comes to technology.

I know these four keys of raising children will help you connect with your children in a more loving way. In this book, the chapters will show you how one of the keys works, offer strategies, to help you guide your scholar, and tell you stories to help you relate to the subject. When finding peace, calm and inspiration, you can see your path in a different way and become enlightened to help your children through their journey. Collecting our angels and then watching them spread their wings and fly on their own is a precious gift that we can all embrace and be grateful. Their qualities of being a scholar athlete will shine through.

Why I'm the Expert in Raising Scholar Athletes

This book comes from my passion of loving and teaching children. I always had a passion toward the education of children and with all my years as a home-mom and educator, I share my knowledge with experiences with children's thoughts, feelings, and temperament.

Being a stay at home mom was one passion, yet I realized a deeper pull toward educating children in schools. I decided to do my graduate work in education by studying to receive my CA credential in multiple subjects for elementary levels K-6. During my first 10 years, I worked as a reading teacher for a Title 1 school. It was my job to increase the reading levels of students.

In addition, I worked with students in special education with IEP's for over four years (Individual Education Plans). I worked in different subject levels along with students on their behaviors, beliefs, and thoughts. Everything I encountered as a teacher, I write in here to help parents become success with their children. Because we aren't perfect people, either are our children. Even athletes have learning disabilities as well as different forms of anxiety to overcome.

My Research Will Help Your Athlete Prosper

By looking into the vestibular and proprioceptive systems as well as the midbrain and how they work, I was able to learn why some students act and have certain movements, suck on their clothes, seem to not pay attention, and hold their pencil too hard. When we monitor our own children, we observe their behaviors and learn what actions to recommend for them at home and school. I've rolled all this information into informative chapters to help parents guide their children to the scholar athletes they want to become.

I began using all the concepts of love, forgiveness, meditation, letting- anger- go, and changing thought patterns along with many other nurturing ideas with my students. These wise thinkers have helped me through my tough times of seeing a student through their vulnerable times in life. Not only was I trying to increase my students' reading levels, but I also aided in their self esteem, negative thinking and their own self realization. I helped them not only practice their reading skills, but learn and practice loving themselves. I share my success stories and offer strategies for parents to help their kids.

It is my calling to write a book to help other mothers and fathers raise children to be independent thinkers and to one day follow their path to their callings. My wish is to pass on information that can help parents who feel they are lost and provide a plan. I want to share my knowledge of teaching little ones. I taught my children to take their passion and one day help others. My hope is that these four keys help you become as successful with your angels.

How This Book Raises Your Scholar Athlete

As you venture through this book, you will find stories, conclusions, purpose, and reasoning to help you on your own journey with your children. They might not seem like angels and you may be feeling like you are living in hell. I promise that if you take these thoughts and theories and work them into your everyday life, you will see the positive changes that you were looking for within yourself and your children.

When reading this book, realize that we are all at different stages of parenting. I'm simply sharing what I did in order to help you create a family unit that can communicate in the most loving manner. All the information learned, through my 18 plus years of working in the field of education and raising my own scholar athletes, is what can help you guide your student to achieving their goal of scholar athlete both mentally and physically. So, flip through the chapters at first and mark the ones that spark an emotion for you and where you feel you need help.

All chapters will be helpful even if you are not exactly at that same point. For example, a family may be adding a sibling and have a need to organize their living space. Even though you have children in elementary school, the organizational aspects will still be helpful and informative and give ideas for your child's age. Remember that the following is not going to happen overnight, but as you stay persistent and learn these four keys that helped me, you will have successful scholar athletes as well as begin to see more happiness, joy and love come into your own heart and life.

Needless to say, by incorporating these four main everyday keys, my daughters are successful, kind, and generous individuals who used their brains for good and not evil. It looked easy as others looked on, but it wasn't. Looks can be deceiving, but if you use the following keys, you will also see your children flourish into responsible individuals who become scholar athletes in college.

Chapter 1

Get Real...
Experience

"Let's get ready to rumble!"

~Michael Buffer

In the famous words of a referee in the wrestling ring, "Let's get ready to rumble!" You are either a new mom, a mom adding another sibling, or a mom trying to get through it all. If you are in any of these stages of a mom, please know that each chapter will help you. You may be past some of these particular stages, but use the information to check and compare how and what you used to create your family environment.

No matter what stage you are in, welcome this information into your heart. Discussing real topics like who does the bills, who feeds the little ones, who has say in bringing up your children, and what sacrifice really looks like is all here for you with the truth. It may sound tough, but let it in, think about the outcomes that can be achieved, and get ready to live a peaceful fun life with your kids.

Your newly created angel is ready to make its appearance but are you? Procrastination is in all of us. Not letting it take over our whole life is the secret. Step away from your laptop, turn your phone to mute, and have a real discussion with your mate on all the important aspects of adding an additional child to your already insane lifestyle.

Devising Your Plan

Start with love for yourself and then love for others. As adults, we usually know what we should be doing, but put it off. We know these important things will better our life, organize our thoughts, and make our journey more comfortable, but feel a wall of fear that keeps us from the thing we should be doing. Take the step to do what has importance in your life and push through with love. Once you see everything in the light of love, everything becomes easy.

The earlier the essential items are discussed out loud with your mate or spouse and assigned, the better. Nailing down in a real conversation and determining who will be responsible for what is essential. Actually, make it an obligation to set a time and date to cover the important aspects. Pick a day to sit in a quiet place, turn off the cell phones, television and all media, sit back and breathe.

Some of the important issues that need discussion are chores, bills, expectations of family members, but more importantly expectations of each other. What you are actually doing is scheduling your life for the future.

Taking time to put these notions in action and tackling them early on is key to less aggravation later on. Doing the right thing is sometimes harder than we think. No one wants to bring up aspects of life that could start bad feelings, but it is necessary to fight through the fear and put these out into the universe.

Who is going to do the bills? Who will do what chores? Paying your bills and keeping your house somewhat clean is necessary. As you get serious, make up your mind to be in charge of your life.

There is always that walk-on-eggshells moment when you bring up the expectations of others. Remember, it is ok to have expectations, but those are your thoughts and not realistic. Your spouse may have the expectation that husband's go to work while wives handle the children at home at all times. In the meantime, you are thinking of all the time you will get to rest and take a walk when they come home to relieve you. In order to avoid a breakdown in communication, be willing to speak up and talk about all these feelings and assumptions.

Without really thinking of the other person or taking into consideration how tired they will be after a long day at work, you are expecting what you want, but not what the other needs. You may surmise that it might warrant some in home help a few times a week in the form of a babysitter or helpful grandparent.

In order that all things stay positive, acknowledging your own expectations and working out solutions, before a crisis unravels, is the best "getting real" session you will ever have and appreciate. You will be so happy that you took the time to delve into these awkward areas and discuss possible solutions.

It sounds so simple, but the best way to organize your future is by creating some quiet space in your home. If it is necessary, ask a family member to look after the angel you already have or hire a babysitter. Discussing out loud and not in a cell phone text is a great first step to peace.

Having a list already made by both spouses would be key but not always realistic in our busy lives. Sometimes, creating a list of things to discuss on the spot is very reasonable.

Tread Lightly

As you begin, approach each area of discussion lightly and be ready to compromise. For example, if the chores of cleaning the house will have to be broken down into small little chores done every few days, then that is what might become the new norm. If you are someone who wants everything done a certain way, be ready to let that go for a while because not everyone will clean as thorough as we want. Be willing to divvy up the toilet cleaning, vacuuming with dusting, mopping, laundry and dishes.

Tell yourself that in time when the children are more grown, you will have the time to clean in a more detailed manner that you enjoy but right now it is time to let certain things go.

Let these issues go for a short time reminding yourself that they will be done to your proper way when time in your schedule lends itself. Having a house raked up and somewhat presentable is the goal when children are young. Putting things away so no one trips and having the essentials cleaned so that no one gets sick is your goal. It is easier to put the sign, "Forgive our mess but we live here," on your door and enjoy your family.

In addition to your expectations of each other, it is vital that you now consider the expectations of your family members. Nothing is worse than having your heart set on something special in your mind and it changes because an in-law had ideas of their own for their grandbaby.

Being part of a dysfunctional family myself, I totally understand that not all couples can have adult conversations with others in their family. However, if you are an individual where you can have these grandparents or aunts/uncles over that live close by to discuss your expectations, wants, and needs, it will be well worth the awkward uneasy feeling. Having them over for some dessert and coffee as a visit with the youngest grandchild/nephew can lead into the discussion.

Stand Up For What You Believe In

It can actually begin by you making statements of what is important to you and your spouse. Keep remarks in a positive way when you speak of things being handled when it comes to your children and their niece, nephew, or grandchild. There isn't any need to create negative vibes or set anything in stone. This can be more of a time to acknowledge your morals, values, and traditions that are important to you and your new family and welcoming any ideas.

Now that my girls are in college and grad school, I look back and regret not standing up for what I wanted with my children more. Many holidays were taken away from me and celebrated at an in-laws house when I simply wanted to celebrate and create my own memories.

Don't get me wrong; once my daughters entered middle school and I entered into my 40's, I was empowered to stand up for me and my ideas. Yes, looking back today with my father in-law now in Heaven, I'm grateful we attended certain holidays. What I'm trying to express is to do your holidays the way you want. While my girls were young, I invited both sets of grandparents to be in our home as my girls came down the stairs to the living room to see what Santa had left. We also created traditions in our home for Thanksgiving as well. I just want to share that because I felt pressured to give up my holiday dreams, I had to experience holidays that were not very kind to me. If you have lived in experiences like this, think about ways to celebrate with everyone but in different ways.

When it came to Thanksgiving and Christmas, I asked for the actual holiday to be spent at home when the girls were young, which is how the day after celebrations began. We would all meet at someone's house with all our leftovers. It was a way to see and include family members on each side, and I began my own home traditions for my girls to remember.

With the girls in college on the east coast during Thanksgiving, I realized how quick the time went and how many of them I had to compromise. As I share my experiences looking back, I want to suggest these options so you can have some wonderful memories and photos to look back on with a warm place in your heart.

Nevertheless, if you already know what kind of in-law you will be up against and don't believe that your wishes will be taken into consideration, be sure to walk through the fear of being uncomfortable. State exactly what your views are in relationship to the baby's celebrations, upbringing, and your new family traditions that are meaningful to you.

Letting the universe hear your wishes will help you feel much better. Be brave and show your under belly. It may help open hearts and minds of others.

Practice Makes Perfect

Practice makes perfect is another wonderful saying that a growing family should heed. As your tribe grows, carry out everyday life with more than one child. Practice having a larger family by practicing with your nieces, nephews, or friend's children.

Make arrangements to watch someone's infant/baby while watching your own during dinner, bath time, grocery shopping, or even play time. Figuring out how to take care of two children is key to being prepared when your bundle of joy makes its entrance. It is imperative that your spouse/mate is also present on one of these occasions. Yes, if you are going to be home by yourself with the little darlings, it is smart to have one of these dress rehearsals by yourself.

Let's be real though, it is mandatory that your better half accompany you on one of these real experience trial runs. While you are experiencing the real deal with having to cook, feed, and diaper one while watching the other, be sure to try certain ways of doing things as well as ask questions. The next chapter, Simplify Your Life, has great ideas and strategies to make your days run smoothly. Moms of more than one have great ideas to share and love to show how they manage through their day.

After you spend time this way, be sure to write down what you learned, different ways to do things, and some of the things that went wrong and how you managed the chaos. I was fortunate enough to receive a mom's journal where I could jot down funny things my children did during a day or my own thoughts. Notes on your Smartphone can work the same way. This would be a great place to write these important items down and carry it in the diaper bag.

Yes, this sounds like a class, yet so well worth it. There really isn't a better way to experience two children at one time than to do it. The more you do it, the better prepared you will be when your angel makes its appearance.

Who knows? By taking the time to babysit for friends to experience the real deal, you will have some time racked up where these friends might be able to take your eldest child to give you some bonding time when the newest baby arrives.

Fear No Evil

Resistance will be your annoying unwelcomed acquaintance at this point. It will be the heavy feeling that you don't want around. The more you put these conversations and real world affairs off, the more it will be on your mind.

Steven Pressfield, an American author of historical fiction and nonfiction, professed, "The pain of not doing it is worse than doing it." We have to take the side of stepping out of our negative egos and really put the important things in our lives first. Putting our priorities in the forefront of our day will help us overcome the resistance. Adopting the idea that we deserve to put our values and beliefs first in our lives is vital. Once you push through and begin doing these things that are important to you and your family, it becomes habit.

Now that you have gotten real with yourself and the people around you, it is time to get real with the things around you. It is time to have the 'get real' talk with your inner being. Your new word will be sacrifice.

Sacrifice Creates Growth

Parents sacrifice every day with their time, money, and self. Giving up special girl nights out, newer items such as cars and appliances, and being room mom will feel like you are living on a new planet because you aren't putting yourself first. Although eliminating some special activities is not wise for your inner peace, be ready to decrease some self enjoyment activities and be ok with it.

It will be that time in your life where you have to begin picking and choosing when it comes to your regular outings. Movie night with friends might happen every other month and group girl trips may have to be put on the back burner. As you tell yourself you can get through a few months of handling two children, you can plan a wonderful lunch date with friends down the line. Even by putting a date on the calendar will be something to look forward to when you are working hard caring for your angels.

Children come with a hefty price tag, but by downsizing the larger ticket items, it can be affordable. Purchasing cars that are 'used' rather than brand new will save you significant coin.

We had both purchased two new cars before we met each other. When the second child came, trying to function in a two door car was becoming a real struggle. As we looked around, we saw the price tags of new cars/SUV's along with substantial monthly payment that came with them. Knowing that we faced future preschool bills, clothing, diapers, and food for these angels down the road, we began looking at used automobiles.

It was a wise choice for us because keeping up with the Jones' was never important to us. Looking back, it was a great learning point for our children. Being in college, they see how expensive it is to be in the real world. They see how keeping up with the Jones' is not productive as they go towards their goals and dreams.

By selecting used items such as cars and appliances, we saved a measurable amount of money and more importantly were able to live within our means. Let's get real, having a used vehicle with cheerios and juice spilled all over is easier to manage when it is cheaper and the payments are easier to swallow.

When high priced appliances are breaking down, it is exciting to look at the newly technological refrigerators, dishwashers, and televisions. Today's machinery is incredible and inviting. However, exactly like the new car, the new appliance will do serious harm to your checkbook.

God's Grace and Blessings

Looking on line, calling senior living facilities, and researching local online garage sales in your neighborhood will find you reasonable items. Letting your friends and work acquaintances know that you are looking for a used appliance is one way we found a dishwasher. A friend knew someone who had a working dishwasher in his garage. He had surprised his wife with an updated quieter version. Fortunately, our friendship was the key to us scoring the used item.

The same thing happened when we were looking for a newer refrigerator. A friend who renovates kitchens was updating someone's kitchen from head to toe including brand new appliances. The appliances she had were already top of the line. Again, because of who we knew, the wonderful woman GAVE us the refrigerator! It was one that had a water and ice dispenser in the door. We were thrilled to receive such blessings in exchange for the time it took me to bake a banana bread.

Remember, whatever you put into the universe, you will receive. We put our faith in our Divine daily. We are always practicing to be grateful for all our blessings we receive along with those coming in the future. You will come to find that as you keep an opened and positive mind no matter what circumstance you are in, your heavenly Father will provide for you. Keeping a positive and thoughtful attitude whether in a good or bad mood will find us with all our wants and needs.

Our paths are already set for us. We need to remember to be

available to others when they are truly in need. So, when you take notice that you are paying your bills month after month with minimal struggle, be sure to give back. It is important to bless those in need because there will be a time when you are in need. On that occasion of hearing that someone is in need, be sure to respond and take action.

As I finished up the bills every month, there were sometimes when I would need a certain amount of money to complete each billing cycle. We were always blessed with checks out of the blue for those amounts needed from some lawsuit connected with our insurance company.

We knew what it was. Some may call it coincidence, but we know that because we did everything we could for our God in the manner in which he has asked, we received our blessings; what we needed. Those were days that we had to practice being in a good mood when things weren't always going our way. We also had to show our true courage and strength by having faith and not letting it slip from our hands.

Trying to live on a small salary in order to be a stay-at-home mom for a while was challenging, but because of our beliefs and compassion for others, He showed His mercy to us time and time again. Staying in peace, keeping up prayers for yourself and others, and remaining centered, you will find your way through this wonderful journey of raising your angels.

Chapter 2

Simplify Your Life

"Life is really simple, but we insist on making it complicated."

~Confucius

Less equals more. I once read that when we allow less expense, less work, and less stuff into our lives, we are also allowing more money, more time and more joy into our daily essence.

When our children are born, they are not thinking about the house they will live in or the car their parents are driving. They are thinking about the love they have inside and the joy they feel being with you.

Finding the least expensive way to see nature's beauty was my goal daily when I stayed at home with my girls. In light of my small funds, I looked for the most beautiful places to view the waves at the beach and at the same time, creating a special moment and space for my girls.

Story of Ki's

I found this restaurant on the east side of the beach strip that had seating up high on the second floor outside overlooking a beautiful view. From those tables, we could see the waves break, the pelicans glide, the surfers ride, and the shell enthusiasts rake. I would order a large smoothie and a toasted baguette each time. After ordering down stairs, we would venture upstairs and my two girls would pick the table for two outside on the veranda and drag another chair to make three.

They would take turns carrying the number on the metal stand and place it on the table. I walked back into the drink area and always filled three small plastic glasses of water and grabbed two more small plastic glasses so I could split the large smoothie into thirds.

As the smoothie and baguette made their arrival, their eyes would grow with the look of delight on their faces knowing that they were going to drink that delicious raspberry elixir. The ritual pouring of the smoothie began by making sure no one received more than the other.

Meanwhile, our baguette was always ordered to be cut into thirds and I would hand them out. They would look at them as if they were being served the most expensive meal on the menu. They would sit quietly looking out to the ocean like one would at a campfire all the while crunching on their toast and slurping their smoothie.

To walk or sit on the beach was one thing, but to be sitting atop a restaurant's lanai savoring every bite of delicious food was such a pleasant feeling. I accomplished what I set out to do and that was to spend time with my girls in a special way. Whenever we were ready to leave, I made sure the girls cleaned their area of any spills and they each took turns leaving the tip. I felt it was important for children to recognize hard work and show their gratitude.

Years later when a close friend came to town, we took them to this same restaurant since it had the best view. Later, my daughters told me that they were wondering why I would take my friend to the place of smoothies and baguettes and not to a restaurant with a more elaborate menu.

As we stepped up to the counter, I began asking my girls what they wanted. I mentioned my choice and a strange look came over their faces. They have other food besides smoothies and baguettes? When did this happen? The looks towards me were both stunning and awkward. Following their realization that this was a full restaurant, I told the story about my limited funds and my way of showing them things from every point no matter the budget. As I heard my own words and remembered those fun times, I enjoyed the accomplished feeling that I practiced what I preached.

I practiced loving life within my means and taught my daughters the same lesson. They actually live it and now laugh about their small excursions at college spending the least amount of money to experience wonderful places when they visit their surroundings. I am happy to report that my girls enjoyed delicious egg burritos with their smoothies at the restaurant near the beach!

Living in this manner was a lesson for me and my children. Sometimes you cannot always get what you want. Sometimes you will only get what you need. They see that it wasn't just a moment in time or a onetime thing either. They have lived in the real world where you only have so much money in your palm and you need to decide how it will be spent. Moreover, they saw the lesson of finances combined with love. I didn't love them less because I only spent so much on them; I loved them more because I gave them all that I had.

Reduce your need to have everything. Untie yourself from the want and attach yourself to the moment. Separate yourself from thinking you need certain things in order to be someone and release the ideas you think make you better or more superior in the world. The world is really what you make of it. The restaurant at the beach clearly shows this practice. Sitting in a prestige restaurant and experiencing such beautiful scenery at the cheapest price shows us that anyone can be anywhere no matter the bill.

Second Hand Rose

As my second pregnancy came closer to delivery date, I remember wondering how in the world am I going to clothe these angels of mine. After seeing how fast my eldest daughter grew, I was nervous about how I was going to find all the different sizes for them.

Once again, when you put ideas into the universe, your prayers are heard and answered. There was a neighbor who had a daughter about five years older than my first born. Whenever she had her daughter clean out her drawers, she would make a call to us, and we would go over with the red wagon and collect the bags of clothes. They loved pulling them out in the living room and trying them on. It was like Christmas morning to them.

As they became older in fifth and sixth grade, they would hear our answering machine with the neighbor's voice and immediately run out the front door and through the parking lot to her condo. They would bring the many bags of clothes up to their room and begin the sorting and fitting. I remember how they would walk down stairs and model their new found outfits. Once again, banana bread baked for our blessing, but now baked by my daughters.

My youngest ended up being the one who baked them. Maybe this was her dream becoming fulfilled? She now works hard on her masters in business with the dream of one day having her own bakery. Maybe this dream came to light all because of a caring and sharing neighbor.

Another wonderful idea for obtaining my girls' clothing was from the thrift stores in town and back home in NY. Back in my hometown, there was a thrift store in the basement of the Catholic Church. My mom would go every week and rummage through the incredible amount of baby onesies and adorable dresses. She would put them in a large box and ship them to me. For the price of one outfit, I received many.

Here in my new town, the churches don't have thrift stores like back home, but we have some in the community. These were the best places to find jeans, toys, or shirts of specific colors for special school activities. How wonderful to find brand names hanging on the hangars for half the price. Once more, we found ourselves being blessed. The universe heard our calls and desires, so God placed our needs in our hands.

In order to give back in our way, we became the neighbor who gave away our girls' outfits to the younger neighbors next door. It is a wonderful feeling to do your part. They would get excited the same way my girls did when they got the call. If they were away or the sizes were too big, we always took our used clothing to the local thrift shops and still do.

Not only do you help others find clothing for a great price, but it helps others with employment. Isn't that why we are all here? Aren't we here to help one another? God says to love our neighbors as we love ourselves. Giving away things that mean something special to us is one of the greatest gifts we can teach our children. We would not only bring our outgrown clothes, but walk around the store and look for some excellent finds. We found our mouse cookie jar and our cherished rolling pin at our local thrift shop.

I was hoping to show my daughters that there are places where they can receive free bread and places to find everyday needs for under a dollar. Now that they are living away from home and attending college, they tell me about the thrift shops they have found.

A Place for Everything

Simplify your life comes in many forms. Having your finances simplified is important, but so is having a well functioning home. Eliminating clutter around your rooms so little one's hands stay safe is significant to their safety. Create areas for their toys in the living room, den or family room. Simply using boxes with decoupage of pretty wrapping paper on the sides or having the children color the sides themselves work wonderfully and at a low cost. At local dollar stores, there are plastic containers for these items also. There are wonderful coffee tables and small chairs available that also have compartments for toys.

When it comes to cooking, the little angels always want to be near us. Safety is always number one so finding an area in your pantry or counter spaces closest to the floor and away from the stove is key.

Storing your plastic Tupperware and storage containers with plastic utensils in this safe place away from flame and heat can be easy access for the children. That way, as you cook, they can pull these out and pretend. This creates another one of those wonderful moments to enjoy with them. Time does fly especially when you are having fun. These times are etched in my mind as some of the best memories I have and bring a smile to my face.

As you set up a place for your containers, think about an area where you can put all the items necessary for the older sibling to manage their own food. For instance, it never fails that whenever you need to change a diaper or feed the new baby, the other child will need a drink or snack.

Everything in Its Place

By simply spending a little time organizing your cabinets and making snacks available, you will be able to teach while giving the Big Brother or Sister a sense of responsibility. In the kitchen, organize a low cabinet with plastic bowls, plates, cups and utensils for the big sibling. Next to this area, create a self storage of snacks where little hands can reach. When those times come up where your hands are full and someone needs a drink or snack, they are available to him or her. If you are worried about having too much food available, be sure to only allow a few things in that area for each day.

We are all aware how bulky and large milk containers are in our refrigerators. Set up a spot in your fridge with milk either in individual Sippy cups or in a smaller pitcher that can be handled with more ease to pour. Of course, it all depends on the age and abilities of the older sibling. This is not only a learning time for them, but a convenience for you.

Allowing your children to get their own drinks and snacks is an essential learning idea. Once you set the rules about when and how much they may get on their own, this becomes a learning experience that sets consistency in their brain. Of course the child should practice asking permission but they should also be able to practice pouring and serving themselves. This can turn into a learning experience of actually serving others as well.

One way to curtail the future spills would be to model pouring and having the child actually practice in front of you. Putting a towel on the table or on the floor near the refrigerator as a table cloth would also act as a great drying agent. As we know, when breast feeding, it is important to replenish your water intake. So asking your little helper to serve up some fresh water to you throughout the day would be a great learning routine. It will help them see they matter in their family and the world around them.

When it comes to snacks, these can be done in a few ways. Some healthy snacks can be purchased in bulk and you can replenish the snack draw available to the older child every day. Producing some healthy snacks that are homemade or purchased from large bulk containers can easily be divided into small baggies or plastic containers with easy flip tops for easy access.

Although your time is really spent constantly taking care of another being whose mind's usually only on eating and sleeping, try to incorporate time to produce nutritious snacks. When cutting up vegetables for meals, cut up a few extra for snacks for both you and your older child.

While you rock the fussy new angel, the older one can bring you a portion of delicious veggies to munch. Include this idea with everyone in the household. As fruit is purchased and brought home, make it a habit of taking time to clean and bag or box some portions into baggies or containers. This is something that can be taught to the other sibling. This takes only a few minutes and will definitely hit the spot when you feel those hunger pains. Having these veggie and fruit snacks available in the fridge will be a source of learning for your older child.

As your older child helps make, eat, and serve these snacks to you and her younger sibling, she's laying the foundations of good eating habits into her brain.

Real Food, Real Good

Consistency plays a big role here. As you practice these good habits, they become reality to your child. Reminding them that good nutrition is an excellent way to stay healthy, they learn by doing. As you model and repeat the goodness of healthy choices, you are creating these learning moments that are so essential to a wonderful introduction into health. Believe me, what you teach your youngster is taken with them to college.

Consistently showing them eating food that grows from the very ground they walk on is invaluable. Like I mentioned previously, it is really what you show and have available to your children that counts. Smoothies and baguettes along with fruits and vegetables every day are foundations to plant in the minds of your children so they grow in the best possible way.

Convenience vs. nutrition is something we all deal with on a daily basis. When it came to feeding my babies unprocessed food when they moved into the solid food stage, I tried to give them homemade every chance I had. This becomes hard especially if you are working and trying to juggle your busy life.

Remember, if you are over booked, begin to change your schedule. You are the one in charge of it. It may only be for a short period of time, but reschedule all church events, family obligations, and school functions until you have more time on your hands.

Recognize that these previous moments do not last forever and it is important to create the best well functioning people possible. Remind yourself this daily. What you put into your child whether it be verbally or by substance, you are in control of the source, amount, and kind. To avoid any possible learning disability in the future, take the time in these few months to display the right choices of food for your child.

Cooking real wholesome food is easy and healthy. All I did was introduce vegetables and fruits to my babies one at a time. I would cook carrots, potatoes, lentils, apples and mash bananas. Once I cooked the vegetable or fruit down to a soft substance, I would simply blend it in my blender. I wouldn't add any salt or sugar. I let my children experience the true taste of the food.

Don't get me wrong, I bought some fruit and jarred vegetable baby food for days when the cooking thing was not going to work. When I did that, I would simply wash and save the jars for the food I made. Life isn't easy so work smart not hard. Keep those dreams alive in your thoughts. Recall and bring to mind all the ideas you had when dreaming of this precious baby. Remind yourself about all the wonderful opportunities you were going to make possible, write them down, and be sure to make them reality.

This is your time to do that now. With all the talk of children with autism and learning disabilities in the news and in the classroom, it is necessary to do everything possible to give your child every fighting chance. Beginning a regimen of consistent healthy eating is the best way to avoid many problems down the line.

As you become better at your baby-food manufacturing, you will try more and more vegetables you have found boring, but now realize the delicious taste. Consistency in nutrition can easily be available as you cook these for yourself and your older child.

Now, we don't want to create the stereotypical dinner table scene where we force our children to remain at the table until all vegetables are eaten. Instead, form your own rules that provide learning with comfort. We would suggest that our children try something at least three times and with only a few bites.

We shared with our children the knowledge that sometimes after three times, people might actually like a certain food. If they truly don't like the item, I made sure I didn't force them to eat it. There will be plenty of vegetables they enjoy as you move through the produce aisles. Simply take note and be sure to cook the ones they eat.

We also maintained that dinner time was not a time to have differently cooked foods. When preparing meals, I made sure there were a few different vegetables to eat like a salad and broccoli. If you didn't care for broccoli, you had to partake in the salad and vice versa. Basically, I used the 70's idea of eating what was provided but on a more loving manner. "You have two choices for dinner, take it or leave it."

Have your children help in the preparing of the meals. They learn what each meal should have to maintain good health. They also become aware how much time and effort goes into making meals. From the washing and cutting to the actual cooking to cleaning up, your child becomes aware that good clean food takes time. When they make it to college and live on their own, they will think back and remember that good food is good for their body.

During my daughter's fifth year of graduate work, she shared a house with others and had to make her own food. Gone were the days of eating at the college dining hall. We were delighted to attend a wedding in the area and to see her house-dorm. Like all college parents, you take them grocery shopping so they have everything they need. As we helped unload her food in her shared kitchen, she showed us how she had a small pot of lentils in the refrigerator as well as chicken individually bagged in the freezer. Believe me when I say they do as we do.

Your Children Are What They Eat

Avoiding the fast food lines and drive thru lanes is very important to their future health. I am not saying that your children will never be given fast food, nor am I saying that you will not find your way to the drive thru lane. What I do want to share is our ability as parents to help our children make the right choices for their future.

If you give a child nothing but chemical based, processed food with no nutritional value, it will end up giving them a life unworthy of the dream you promised them. It is your job to show them how to stay healthy. It isn't for the schools to do. We must take this seriously, since their ultimate destiny is based on their wellness.

A key to becoming a successful individual is to monitor your body's intake and make sure that every cell in your body has a fighting chance. Of course a taste of a McDonald's fry is not going to put you in the hospital. Be aware that having these treats rarely is a good model for your children.

You will see that once you present good food to your children, they will have their own reactions down the line on how the processed food makes them feel. Those times can be a learning moment. Discussing the difference in the way their stomach feels when eating good food vs. processed can warrant great conversations.

These conversations with my own children came up because I gave them clean food. Throughout their elementary days, they would opt out of a school lunch because they didn't like the taste or how it made them feel. They saw how some foods were loaded with salt and fat. Growing up with healthy food really planted a seed in them.

Even now at college, they say that they mostly picked from the salad bar and healthy soups and avoided the soda machine. They noticed the salt and sugar in some foods offered, so as athletes they were aware that their muscles needed nutrition and not empty calories. It made a difference in their lives.

When you make the right choices at the grocery store, have them help you prepare the meals, and consistently demand the best food at your dinner table as a rule. In turn, you will have educated children who make the right choices as they grow and mature. When you take the time to incorporate these learning experiences and model the correct way to be successful, you will end up with awesome outcomes.

Consistency is very crucial here. If you skip the whole idea of teaching your child daily how to nourish themselves, you will have children who will not be able to become everything they are supposed to be. We already have our journeys spelled out and mapped out for us. He already knows what our passions are and what direction we will go. Don't we want to send our angels down their path as healthy as possible?

If we don't have the proper knowledge and background to take on our journeys, we will fall short of our dreams. It is important to retain the knowledge and practice it in order to be successful. To be consistent in something is to retain it. We must practice this daily.

Becoming a successful individual in life, where you not only move forward toward your dreams but help others on your way, takes a lot of hard work and great effort. Because you are a mother who puts these concepts and keys first and foremost in the mind of your children, you will see it every step of their way.

Taking the extra time to educate at every possible moment in your child's life is the best way to help mold and form the best imaginable person. Their success of becoming a caring and wonderful individual is really in your hands. Take the time to teach your children well, and you will see them in turn treating themselves well.

Chapter 3
Stick to a Schedule

"It requires a minimum of 21 days for an old mental image to dissolve and a new one to jell."

~Dr. Maltz

Dr. Maltz was a plastic surgeon in the 1950's and saw this happen for his patients time and time again. After a minimum of 21 days, his patients became very comfortable with their new face. Years later, many self help books changed this time line to a definite 21 days whereas Maltz's findings used the word minimum.

Soon after, everyone began stating that change takes 21 days whether it is exercise, diet or something else. I mention this to help you understand how long change can take when we are working with our angels and trying to reshape and mold their schedule. Although it can take longer than 21 days, we want to put our focus on the different aspects of change and realize that once we are in the changed behavior, it is a very rewarding feeling.

Think about your schedule of getting up and getting ready for work. If you examine it, you will see that you probably do things in the same order: take a shower and then brush your teeth. Maybe you drink your coffee before you do anything. When you realize you do things in the same fashion, this is your routine. It is usually set up by you with some important things you want to happen in the morning to make it enjoyable for you.

Schedule the Chaos

The same thing goes for a house with angels floating around. It is necessary for a schedule to be created around the individuals' wants and needs. Children actually strive better in a schedule. They manage their days better if their day is predictable. When they have a schedule in place, it becomes their normalcy. Keep this clear and remain firm as parents. Your children sticking to a schedule helps shape their independence and is a great way to practice following directions at school and later in life.

I remember as I was growing up in my 20's, I would be late for everything. Staying on schedule was my way of playing beat the clock. I'd be late for doctor appointments, parties, and I'd drive myself crazy every morning by leaving for work right at the last possible moment that would have me sprinting into the office two minutes after eight.

I distinctly recall hitting the office door so hard that the bell sounded like it was coming to break through the glass. I'd get a hello from the secretary attached with a face of discontent. I would try to walk to my desk as casual as I could and acted as if I was just about to talk to the next high paying client. Looking back, I recall those moments of trying to catch my breath at the same time I would try to place a call so no one could verbally acknowledge my tardiness.

Scheduling For Security

I think I finally turned it around after an angel from Heaven kept me from a horrible accident. It took the scare of my life to make me finally stop my continual rushing. It was another voice speaking to me in a way that it wasn't someone nearby, rather from my soul. I took the advice of turning ahead my alarm clock and house clock by twenty minutes. As I started experiencing my own calmness and the serene looks from others around me, I knew it was the answer. I took the time to feel the soothing and peaceful reaction my body felt and realized that this is the change I needed. Being young, we think we have all the time in the world and we are immortal. A schedule free from stress and anxiety is the way to live safe and secure.

We always want our children to be safe and secure. Schedules are the best way to keep them feeling that way. Routines are necessary to keep them feeling protected. When a child's daily routine is predictable, they have a sense of feeling snug as a bug. If they know what to expect, they become little people with more confidence. In turn, they begin to do things out of habit. Good habits, of brushing their teeth after eating, cleaning their own dishes, and getting their own lunch boxes and bags ready by the door, are the best habits to push.

Growth Comes From Scheduling

Every child wants television, games, or music playing while they prepare for their day. Putting your foot down and not allowing technology before they are ready for their day is the most important rule in a schedule. This not only creates a peaceful morning for all to enjoy, but also reminds our children that their own thoughts and quiet thinking exist and should be tended to daily. Use television viewing as a reward, however remember that teaching our youngsters about silence and enjoying quiet is not only healthy, but will be a huge part of whether your child succeeds in learning.

The research on noise and the effects it has on our children's brains is enough to stop anyone in their tracks. Because our infants' brains are developing at an alarming rate, the environment we chose to create phenomenal minds is the secret.

Back in the 1960's and 1970's, it has been learned that children did not sit in front of a television until the age of four years. Now, it is four months! If our children's brains are developing at such a fast rate during these early months and we give them the wrong sustenance, we have only ourselves to blame when it comes to the epidemic of ADHD (Attention-Deficit/Hyperactivity Disorder). As parents, we must be the ones in charge of what our children eat and view, and we must create the best learning environment for every minute of our children's lives.

The 21 Day Habitual Method

You might be thinking, "Sure, I'll just cut technology out of their life in the morning and watch all heck break out!" I understand and remember how our children ranked their wants that were important to them. Start their new schedule of 'no technology' in the mornings by weaning them.

The week before the new rule comes into place, put out the warning in many different ways. As your children are getting ready for their day and possibly watching television in the morning, remind them that starting the following week, there will be no television when getting ready for school. State your intention and back it up very calmly by relating it to the love you have for their brain. You will hear moans and groans, but tell yourself that is to be expected.

In addition, in the evening as they approach bedtime, this is another good time to present the change in their schedule. For example, this would be a good time to suggest a plan of laying out the next day's clothes in order to independently get ready for school and to receive a reward.

As they lay out their breakfast cereal bowls with spoons and juice cups, they learn the importance in their independence. If you remind them if they selected their outfits the night before and set the table for breakfast, this would allow them to be organized. In turn, they receive time to watch a few minutes of television/game time before leaving for school or daycare as a reward.

Remind them it doesn't always mean TV will be used. Maybe music or images and audio will inspire that day. As you do this, you are letting them get adjusted to the new idea of the upcoming change.

While they are getting ready for their day in the morning, this would be a good time to state some planning ideas.

For example, you may remind them that organizing their backpacks in the evening is a great way to lessen the hassle in the morning. Having them organize, find, and place their own supplies in their backpack such as jackets and books, really helps them become more responsible with their own items.

This will not happen overnight and the struggle will be real for about a few weeks, but realize that this two to three week transition is better than having an ongoing daily struggle in the mornings. When you think about it, this is straight out of the strategy book that teachers use at the beginning of the school year. While their students are practicing being organized, the teacher is verbally reminding them of the benefit.

Remind yourself that this is a learning process. Find the good things they do and reward them by complimenting them. Give them your wonderful rewards of hugs and kisses for their efforts. Keep using a firm will. Have the words "Be Consistent" on your bathroom mirror, refrigerator, and microwave. It is a good idea to remind them that this is the new schedule and going back to the old way of watching television is not going to happen. Take a stand the night before by verbalizing your intention and showing persistence every morning by sticking to your plan.

In reality, children like to see where the line is drawn so they know how far they can move in the acceptable behavior and their boundaries. Think of how wonderful your mornings will be when you put the work into those 21 days. There is a light at the end of every tunnel and you will be happy that you took the time to create such a peaceful space in your day.

Perfect Timing

Consistency is a great way to stay on a schedule. It is also a key to your child becoming a leader. By not deviating or changing your course because of the frustration of your child, they will learn the important aspects it takes to have self discipline.

Setting limits and teaching our children how to live within these limits is what will elevate your child to becoming someone who is successful and a leader. As we show and guide them on how to deal with their own wants and the pain of not getting their way, we are actually molding their ability to realize their impulses. Some actions such as grabbing something they want or getting attention from a loving parent, because of a good choice they made, might be what are guiding their direction.

In the process of recognizing their wants and needs, they become individuals who learn self control. By not giving into everything your child wants, you are in turn saving them from the life of becoming an individual who comes off as spoiled or someone who gets whatever they want.

When your child becomes angry and upset when they don't get their way, remember every time you are firm, you are bringing your child closer to being a person who can tolerate frustration and manage themselves. Since we see how frustrating our days can sometimes be, we want to help our child learn the necessary tools to maintain their frustration and make good judgments with the ability to think for themselves.

Frustration and Inconvenience

If you consistently cower down when your child becomes angry or frustrated when they don't get their way, they will become a little terror. By letting their frustration and tears control how you set their limits, you are only doing a disservice. It is one of the hardest parts of being parent. Hearing them breakdown and cry for not getting their way sends that shock wave from your brain, to all your nerves and back to your head creating a massive stress headache.

At that moment, we always want to give our child what they want to ease their frustration. But by constantly letting them control all their wants, you aren't teaching them how to set limits for themselves. As they practice living through the pain of not getting everything, they learn there are limits and also learn how to live within them. You will experience fits and meltdowns, but keep calm and carry on. We know as adults, getting everything you want is not how the world operates. Know that your actions taken now are actions of love helping to create the successful adult.

Being consistent in your actions as a parent creates children who can live within limits and later set them for themselves. A successful child is one that can see the limits, control their frustration, and have the ability to think for them. If you plan on helping your child on the journey toward attending college, these are important aspects that you want your child to carry out in their everyday lives. When they are on their own, you don't want to worry that they cannot make simple judgment calls such as drinking alcohol or taking drugs and skipping classes. Knowing that they can make smart decisions on their own is your goal.

Keep this in mind while you deal with their tantrums and working through their grief. If you have the end result in mind, it will help remind you why you are doing all this work. You will be sitting with your child again and again while they are having their meltdown, and you will be explaining in a calm manner why they can't have something they want.

It's within this moment of complexity that they are experiencing where they learn to grow. Bill Eckstrom points this out so well in his TED Talk, "Why Comfort Can Ruin Your Life." Complexity is the point where we learn how to sit in our dilemma and then venture forward. Keeping our children in a continuous state of order and comfort will prevent them from growth.

Deep inside you know that by taking this time, you are actually showing love. You are taking a small step toward your child's success and seeing to it that they are on their way to becoming a leader later in life.

Bed time will be a very tough time forming your family's schedule. Because some families are apart for most of the day and only get to spend a few hours together for dinner and family time, there's not a lot of time for everyone to be connected. Creating special time with bath and reading routines is well worth helping your children to be well-balanced.

Consistency Relates To Success

Consistency and routine are important parts to make your schedule work like a well oiled machine. Including things that everyone enjoys is very important. Using calm music while preparing meals can be fun. Keep in mind that too much background noise is not the environment for growing brains.

Letting everyone have a job and setting a calm environment alleviates stress. Include a bath time of a certain amount of time easily kept with the touch of our phone timers. In order to keep bath time relaxing, only use the phone for the timer and leave all other apps closed. Singing together or telling stories makes bath time fun.

Picking out favorite books to read at bedtime creates a lot of enjoyment and helps both parent and child feel connected. This is a time to connect with your child's favorite topics and interests. Keep consistency every night by including these traditions.

Remember to leave the office and work problems at work. Practice living in the now. Allowing yourself to relax and de-stress is crucial to your well-being. Eckart Tolle, a spiritual writer and listed as the 2011 most spiritually influential person in the world, once said, "Realize deeply that the present moment is all you have. Make the NOW the primary part of your life."

I believe he is teaching us that we should live in the present moment more than thinking of the past or the future. Having control of the thoughts of our mind can give us awareness of our true self. This practice, of living in each moment at bath time and bed time reading, allows us to focus on the most important things in our life. Yes, working and making a living are important, but practicing to live in each moment is a wonderful way to experience life fully.

While we are in the frustrating cycles of our children's age, we may want to discontinue this new change in schedule and go back to the old ways. Before you do, think about all the work you have done, all the days you have survived, and mostly all that your children have learned. It would be a big disservice to go back to the old ways.

They are just that, they are old ways. Done and gone. Teach your children it is not ok to go back to the unsuccessful ways. Realize that you are the one in charge. Be the "boss" in charge who does it with kindness, sincerity, and love.

Mark Neppo, author and poet who has been teaching spirituality for over thirty years, once stated, "We need to give up what no longer works and find new ways of being that keep us close to what matters."

What matters to parents is that their children grow, thrive, and learn in the best possible environment. Being consistent, not giving up, and remaining steadfast to the end belief, will guarantee that you cross that finish line of creating that environment where success radiates.

This environment is for the good of the parent as well. Being in a space where we all feel a sense to flourish helps regenerate our own mind and body to be at its best. Putting in the long hours of teaching your children how to function in the best environment at the best of their ability is sacred.

Sacred is the thing that is most important to us such as the serenity area of a house, or the room in which we write or read. When we give up something that is close to us, like our time and emotions, for something that is sacred and means so much to us like an environment of peace, this is truly sacrifice. This time spent is sacred and worth it. Remember, Mark Neppo would say no experience is wasted.

Creating this schedule is going to come with inconvenience. These inconveniences are going to come in the form of you, as the parent, giving up your own time on the laptop, TV, and reading time while the child works through their consequence of losing a privilege. As these schedules are established, you will have to take the time to sit with these angels during their times of refusal.

They will refuse to do what they know is right and try to use their tears and frustration in the form of tantrum to get their way. Be sure to skip to Chapter 9, *Be Friendly, Not Their Friend*, for step by step strategies for rewards and consequences.

Since you will have rewards and consequences set up to help negotiate the behavior, you will find yourself sitting with them and reading their books, playing with their toys, and playing or teaching them a new board game when they refuse to follow their schedule and ultimately lose their media time.

Reward and Recognition

Rewards are the best and most positive way to motivate a child's behavior. But when children behave poorly, a consequence attached to their favorites in their everyday life will be most effective. Inconvenience is going to be felt during the consequence. Parents create consequences but must be sure to follow up. When a consequence is not performed to its fullness, children will not learn from their bad choices. We do not want to punish a child in order to have them feel pain. What we want to accomplish is for the child to choose his behavior, become aware that their choice has a consequence, live through the consequence, and learn how to become a better, stronger, and more secure individual.

During their fallout, teaching them how to move through their consequence is fundamental. Teaching our children how to feel the mood that connects with a consequence is an important part of growing. When you model with them, such as playing their favorite game instead viewing television, it will become a part of their everyday life. They will learn that consequences are not the end of the world, and they will also be practicing to better themselves.

When in the midst of a consequence, be sure to do it whole heartedly. Giving the consequence of no television and having the child in the same room as you view your show on the television or laptop is not genuine. Be the parent of honor and be ready to rearrange your own schedule and days to accommodate the child's consequence.

If the repercussion is not followed through, the child will learn that their behavior can be controlled by their emotions and your unwillingness to see through to the end. During the repercussion of losing their privileges on their technology devices, remind them of their bad choice and help them to learn from them. Offering them choices to make when they find themselves in certain situations is helpful to our angels.

Chapter 4

Catching Some ZZZ's

"The wise parent doesn't stop loving because the shushing to calm didn't work, the wise parent loves anyway, because whether the child can hear it or not, the screaming child needs love the most."

~Matt Kahn

Love is all you need. These are the Beatles' famous words from a song of theirs. It is also the answer to what you need when you are helping your angel find their sleep sweet spot. It will be your best friend during this anxious time for all. Put it first as you find your way and as you soothe your angel. Along with love, add the key scheduling and pour a glass of red. It will feel like a long ride, but you will come out of this smiling.

Scheduling means taking a series of events and creating a plan to be done in order for something important to be carried out. Sometimes, the best way for a good turnout is to use a timetable. This is needed when creating a calm, quiet, and peaceful bedtime. It has been found that children need at least nine and a half hours of sleep a night for optimum growth and their best immune system. After reacting to all their curiosity during a day, our little ones need to regenerate and refuel. Their bodies need to rest and prepare for another full day of running, climbing, and learning.

When creating their bedtime routine, parents must take into account their sleeping environment. It is crucial that a child's sleep area be cool and quiet. Consistency is the key here for your child to receive the proper amount of sleep. Creating rules and sticking by them is essential. Using a method that fits your anticipated outcome needs practice and firmness with your rules, but offering flexibility to keep your peaceful climate.

There are many ideas, methods, and styles that people use when creating a sleep schedule for their children. Most important is that the schedule meets the child's needs. The most significant advice recommended is put your child to bed when drowsy and not asleep. When your child falls asleep in this manner, you are teaching your child to fall asleep on their own. This is called self soothing. As our child's brain grows, it not only learns language, speech, and making right choices, but the brain develops on the knowledge it learns and the practice of sleeping. When a routine is created and followed, the child learns how to put themselves to sleep.

Culprits of Sleep

There are modern aspects that affect our sleep. Many aspects in a child's day can deter them from achieving the necessary sleep they need to be healthy. Caffeine and screen time are two of the biggest culprits of negative quality and quantity of sleep that a child receives.

Most children between the ages of five and twelve receive nine and a half hours of sleep whereas in actuality experts state that they should be sleeping ten to twelve hours of sleep. Dietary intake should not include caffeine. It is known that nearly three quarters of school aged children consume caffeine with 27% being preschoolers. Researchers found that caffeine has a negative impact on children's sleep. They raise the fact that children who consume caffeine receive less sleep than those who partake in the feign energy.

Exposure time of any computer device right before bed is associated with inadequate sleep. Children experience delayed onset as well as shortened duration of sleep when they view these devices right before closing their eyes. This was found in 90% of those researched. Research shows that children viewing television at bedtime have shortened sleep time. I was amazed to find the percentage of youngsters who have televisions in their bedrooms.

Once investigated, I found that 30% of preschoolers had televisions in their bedrooms with 43% of school-aged children having the sets in their sleep space. More shocking was that 18% of infants and toddlers had televisions in their bedrooms. These are incredibly scary facts since sleep is one of the most important factors for a child's overall brain development.

It is important as the parent to nip these in the bud. Parents should only let their children consume water or 100% juice as their liquids for the day. Of course, if your toddler is in the milk intake stage, by all means, be sure that your little one gets enough. Teaching children what certain substances can do to their bodies would be very enlightening for both the parents and child.

Technology should not have a place in the décor or in the routine for bedtime. Because we want to create a peaceful environment in our house from morning through night routines, stand your ground and model your beliefs to your child as you both learn more about technology vs. sleep. In the upcoming technology chapter, television and screen time are the worst things that tip our angels' halos off their heads due to lack of sleep.

When bedtime starts to resemble a meltdown on aisle #3 at the grocery store, it is time to get serious about creating a bedtime routine that eliminates screen time, any form of caffeine or sugar, and create a calming environment. My eldest daughter never had a problem with bedtime, but the younger daughter did at about the age of 8 months.

Even though we had a schedule in place, she would enjoy all the fun parts like bath play, story time, and hugs and kisses. As soon as we would turn out the lights, she would cry and want to be picked up. We learned about the CIO method or cry-it-out approach. I observed it executed by a well-renowned nanny and noticed how well it worked!

The CIO Method

According to a study published May 24, 2016, in the journal *Pediatrics of Australia*, researchers have found that babies allowed to cry it out at bedtime do not suffer any more signs of stress that babies using any other method of falling asleep. Michael Gradisar, an associate professor and clinical psychologist at Flinders University in Adelaide, Australia, performed a study using two methods of putting babies to sleep: one where they cried it out- CIO, and the other method of delaying their bedtime later and later to help them fall asleep quicker-"bedtime fading".

He found out that the babies that went to bed on the CIO method did not suffer a higher level of stress hormone, cortisol, than the "bedtime fading" method. It is important to state that during the CIO method, neither parent nor caregiver can touch, pick up, or give the baby any physical attention. The parents need to avoid responding quickly to the baby's cry.

We used the CIO method for our youngest when she was having a hard time putting herself to sleep. After bath time and story time, we told her it was bed time. We stated we were going to bed and we were not going to come back in to pick her up or give her any toy, water, or bottle. Be sure to remind the child that bed time is a time to sleep not a time for play.

When the crying begins, it is important to stay away and let the crying occur. At this point, the most important advice I can give is to model peace and love. It will feel very uncomfortable listening to their cries. Let some time pass, approximately ten minutes, before you peak your head in to start their sleep lesson. Calmly and with a smile, tell your child you will see them in the morning. State that it's bedtime for everyone, and slowly close the door. By avoiding picking them up, they learn that their crying doesn't lead to being picked up at bedtime.

We waited another ten minutes before entering. In a calm voice, we would say good night and tell them how much we loved them. This reminds them that you'll see them in the morning. Once again, you've reassured your child and teaching them the routine of sleep time.

Consistency Counts

Consistency counts here. Believe me, I remember wanting to go in, pick her up, and hug her tears away. I would let my guilty thoughts get the better of me. I had to remember that every night I did this, the closer she would be to sleeping without crying. It did take about a week, yet you will notice that you can go a longer period of time before peaking in to use your voice to calm. After about the second night, you will notice the crying becomes less.

Showing that you can remain calm, even though they are very upset, will be the lifeline you are looking for during this awkward and uncomfortable time. It will feel like an eternity when you realize that only five minutes has gone by, but stick with your consistency. Know ahead of time that it will take at least a week of feeling stressed, but keep calm and carry on. As bedtime comes closer, replace your stressed thought each day within a positive one.

Practice consistency the same way you did during their consequences, creating their schedule, and during their bad behavior. Put a smile on your face! You've just consistently modeled to your children that what you say is the rule. As you continue to stick to your plan, your children see you mean business. They will see you as the one monitoring their behavior and the one in charge of handing out of rewards and consequences.

Moving through the cry-it-out event is difficult, so remain firm. You will feel your blood pressure skyrocket and your heart beat faster. You might want to scream yourself. It is merely a stage they go through so trust in that knowledge. Here are some helpful hints.

Use a soft voice, remind your child that it is bedtime, tell them you love them, and you will see them in the morning. At this beginning point, love will be your best friend. As they cry out, state that love is around the child. Love will conquer the negative feelings. Use it to wrap yourself when you begin to feel the tension build each night. This might be a good time to meditate on the word love after the baby is put down to bed. It's cheaper and saves on calories from a glass of wine. Breathing into and out of the word love can help put you into a peaceful place. Like the Beatles said, "Love is all you need."

It takes a good four days to a week to work through this process; however you will see their crying occur less as you stay consistent. You are creating a new environment of calm and peace at bedtime. They will in turn change their habit of crying and replace it with self soothing and self calming.

Soothing Sleep Techniques

Offering some self soothing tips for your child can be wonderful techniques through this stressful time. They can also be used when other stressful times come up. Since we are only interested in our children returning to their relaxed self and reclaiming their self control, parents might want to model some self soothing techniques before bedtime. These techniques can be anything from breathing exercises, practicing relaxation from head to toe, holding and cuddling a favorite stuffed animal, and taking a mental vacation.

Provide a time to practice each approach and teach the skills so they can use them for a later stressed moment. Realize that they will one day use this as they live in their dorm. Demonstrating the steps of breathing and counting slowly with slow breaths is a wonderful way to start. Model it to your child by feigning a stressful time and using breathing to return to a calm state. In addition, along with your child, practice the art of relaxation from head to toe.

Display with your child how to travel from their head to their toes by feeling each part of their body. Adding a humming tune may reveal another gentle element. Every child has a favorite stuffed animal, blanket or blankey. Share with them your secret calming techniques that helped you feel tranquil when you were young.

Lastly, using the technique of taking a mental vacation sometime during the day may be the answer for your angel to drift off to sleep. On paper with crayons, illustrate the steps of drawing a magical place either real or fantasy for a vacation. Be sure to bring out all the important aspects and details of their special place. By bringing these details to life, you can help remind your child to picture these during their bedtime.

Remember, these self soothing techniques are not going to miraculously work the first try. Picking one at a time and seeing how they respond is probably a good idea. As a parent, you know what types of interests your child has, so use the ideas you feel will help them.

Patience to Calm the Savage Beast

Patience will need to be your best friend. Know in your heart that within a few days, your child will learn these new ways of feeling calmer at bedtime and the crying will alleviate. It is important to be the cheerleader for yourself during these tense moments.

Think back to all the tense times that you worked through when they were infants and remember this is only a small moment in their lives. Understand that your knowledge, patience, and consistency to do right by your children exist from God. Reach into your soul and know that the presence of His divine love is all around.

As you experience work events, these relaxing methods may be enlightening for the parent. Practicing these concepts for yourself can only help you return to a stronger parent.

Calm the Mind

As your scholar athlete hits the books, you'll find them staying up later than usual. Be sure to intervene before the lack of sleep begins to interrupt their daily lives.

Because middle school and high school is so much more demanding than when we were in school, the pressure is put on our children with the rigorous work load. Adding this to their hours of practice with their sport, it can become an overwhelming sight.

Nowadays, there are many different drinks that offer the ability to stay awake. Linking this to the fact that they need their body as healthy as possible to continue in their sport, find and offer more nutritious methods.

Melatonin can be taken in the evening a few hours before sleep. By adding scheduling in here, it's important to model and teach them how to create a schedule at the end of their day to enjoy the best sleep. Remember to speak out with your middle schooler or high schooler that over doing it with a lack of sleep can create chaos.

It's important to remind these upcoming NCAA competitors that they are not allowed to have certain supplements that can affect their play. Division I athletes are tested often. It's better to be safe than sorry.

Because of all the pressures that come along with being a scholar athlete, this is a time to help them create a portion of their day to grounding themselves. It can help them realize that they need to create a life that includes fun. By offering this advice, it will help them later in college. They will learn how to implement music, fun, and nature into their lives. Since colleges are seeking more well-rounded individuals, this is a great time to start.

Chapter 5

From One Mother to Another

"Have patience with all things, but, first of all with yourself."

~Saint Frances de Sales

As one mother to another, you will struggle with the whole idea of who you really are as you guide your children in their journey. With all your attention on helping them achieve their goal of becoming a scholar athlete and play their sport in college, you feel that you have lost yourself. The ideas and directions that you thought were going to be yours change. It can be a frightening place. This is a time to dig deep into yourself and remember who you are and what you are at that moment.

As a new mother barreling down this journey with kids, this is the time where you'll be doing nothing but counting to ten and praying. My best gifts are find a quiet place for some alone prayer time and learn to release your ego.

Joyce Meyer and Matt Kahn helped me in these areas. They have great videos online. Park yourself during nap time or soccer practice and take advantage of their wonderful words.

Because we are new apprentices and inexperienced, our ego tries to make us better than we think we are. These future scholars bring with them gifts of knowledge from heaven that ends up helping all of us. Just the same, you bring your unique gifts of being a mother, too.

Picking up a book at Barnes and Nobles or researching articles from the internet may be your library to access and learn how the mind of your angel works. Attending a parental group or class may be another avenue for you to seek and educate yourself on the brain waves of your little one.

Of course you have all the gifts from God such as righteousness, patience, wisdom, faith, and healing. In the Bible, 2 Peter 1:3 says," His divine power has given us everything we need for life and godliness through our knowledge of him who called us by his own glory and goodness."

Keeping Your Mind Clear

Our wonderful children were given to us as a gift from God. We must cherish them and treat them as if they are God because God is already inside your angel.

An old ad comes to mind from Calgon where the mom, in a struggling moment yells, "Calgon, take me away!" All mothers and fathers will feel that at one time or another. A way to survive this crazy stage in your life is all up to what you think. It's all about what you are thinking and feeling.

A wonderful example is a question for all to answer. Do you want to be in the throes of drama including feelings of anger, sadness, and negative thoughts or do you want to feel powerful, happy, with the feelings of joy and comfort? It is all up to what thoughts you have in your mind.

If you get in touch of your thoughts, you can meander with the help of meditations and prayers to God or angels. Dig down deep and think about what you want for your life and your children. Focus upon positive ideas and outcomes that will help you manifest a positive life.

It is important to take control of your actions. Think about, not necessarily who to blame for your actions, but acknowledge the feelings coming up and how you can create the life you want. If you think about all things in a positive way, you can see all your experiences as a way to learn a lesson. I know, it sounds too good to be true but it is. By learning how to manifest your positive life, you need to align your thoughts to the ideas that serve others.

As a parent, you want your children to be safe, secure, and successful. In order to manifest these ideas, you must start to look around, live in awareness of the present, and look for the signs to guide you.

I remember feeling guided day after day when I was home with my children. I would listen and simply follow what I heard from my angels or guides. I remember being pulled to a library, when my children were very young, to write a book on raising children. I can recall the feelings of comfort, being validated for my ideas, and positive ideas whirling around me. As I think back, I can see that there were no negative thoughts, actions, or drama around me.

Although I did have a guide suggest that I write down all my ideas and store them for later, I listened and now see that my writing was always suppose to happen. After seven years of being home with my children, I went back to work. I found myself working in a new school that took me past the same library where I began writing years ago. It was as if my angels were now guiding me to begin what I started.

Each time I became silent in my actions and listened or looked for signs, I have been guided toward what I've always wanted to manifest. While being with my children at home, I knew this was the most important time for them. I knew the information about a child's brain and how significant the first five years were for growth. I had the thought to educate in a fun way, but I had to find my quiet place in my heart and listen. Be sure to look for yours.

Love Comes in Many Colors

One great idea was color day. I did this every week as both girls were preschool toddlers; one year old and a three year old. I would pick a color for the day and then incorporate everything towards that color. For example, if the color was yellow, we would wear the color yellow, buy yellow fruits and veggies of that color, practice writing the word yellow, and do art projects using crayon or paint in yellow.

It gave my children a chance to see that specific color in the world. We would point it out to each other everywhere we went from home to the park. Since the produce store always gave away free balloons, we would get a balloon that represented our color day.

Even though they were only preschool toddlers, they would practice finding the different letters of yellow in baby books. I would show them the letter on a card or they would write the letter in finger paints, sand, or on paper with pencil.

Skimming through magazines to find the color was also fun. Not only would they practice focusing on the pages and using their visual learning strategies, but they would practice their kinesthetic strategies of actually turning the pages of a magazine. This was great way to develop the use of their muscles in their tiny fingers.

It made the day exciting! We would try new fruits and old favorites in that color. It helped them venture off from the security of what was familiar to what was new. They will have new things and changes in their lives. As a result, trying new things helps children became familiar with the feeling of change as a positive one and not one to run from. If the new vegetable was not appetizing, we would have fun in the knowledge that we tried something new.

Every Moment is Important for Knowledge

While visiting the park or going on a beach walk, I would show the color, even if they were very young infants. With just a point and simple wording, you help them learn. This was a great exercise for their brains when listening to specific words and then repeating them.

I believe because I did this on a daily basis, without my attention on a cell phone or other object, my girls progressed through school easily. They had no need to attend a speech class or social group. Because they practiced speaking and talking with others by using their words on a daily basis, they flourished through school. This isn't to say that if your child has a speech problem that it was your fault. By no means is that true. However, having them practice speaking and conversing helps them in these areas.

Watching so many moms putting all their attention on their phone, book, nook, or tablet, worries me. As a special education teacher, I see so many children who have speech and language problems which could have been corrected and supported while they were toddlers.

Being in the moment with your child is one of the most important things any mother can do, yet many choose not to. Be the mom you always knew you could be. Use the strategies of scheduling on you to help become more present. Listen to your angels, help develop the brain of your child, and enjoy every monumental step with a smile.

Mistakes Are Merely Lessons

Mistakes will happen and you will feel as if you know nothing. Within these moments of mistakes, look deeper and find your lesson. Mistakes as a parent are inevitable, however they make you better. Realize that your job now is to adjust to the morals of your family. Begin to seek balance. Recall the foundation your family rules were made from, and start to adapt back to the love and honesty that was set in place originally.

Immediately push through, think positive thoughts, and simply breathe. It is a known fact that our minds can only concentrate on one thought at a time. When you combine that with the practice of breathing in and out continuously for eight seconds while concentrating on a positive thought, you can return to your peace and the feeling of God inside you.

After you breathe, remind yourself to do good works. Stay positive, stay open, and stay calm because your gifts are already in you. Take the time to place yourself into that very moment and smile. Notice your heart beat, notice your breathing, and notice the space in which you dwell.

From there, do everything to the best of your ability. Avoid any negative thoughts that might try to break through your peace. Replace these thoughts with positive ones. As soon as you start to recall any past drama or hurt, shake those thoughts right out and bring to mind your many blessings.

Our angels come to us in all forms. Not all angels become scholar athletes, world renowned physicists, or even the world's greatest teachers. They come to us with their lessons through the way they show up. Our angels may come without sight, but they will only help us to see ourselves and the world around us better. Some angels will come to us missing limbs, but that will be our lesson to notice our triumph through our faith, and endure living in a different way from most.

Angels come filled with their love, lessons, and wisdom to teach us why we exist. As we travel this road and allow others to join us, we receive the most wonderful gift ever; we receive the honor of escorting our angels through their journey as we learn how strong, loving, and brilliant we truly are. Focusing on the journey and being sure to learn every lesson is our calling.

Certain people will see your journey in a different light and move away from your energy. That is perfectly fine. As you put your positive energy out into the universe, you will see how much positive energy you attract.

As you stay in the light and surround yourself in the blanket of all God's gifts you possess inside, you will see that

God only allows those who can help to remain near us. If you notice close friends and so called family members suddenly leave your circle that is God. As Matt Kahn states continuously, "Whatever arises, love that." If that's what's happening in your life, love it and let it happen.

Love where you are. If certain things around you are negative and you are not in control of it, love it. When you are having sad feelings and unsure where they are coming from, plainly love it. Put love first and the rest will follow positively. Love is not negative. It is the light that helps us to see clearly.

As I look back, I recall feeling overwhelmed from all the minor details that had to be taken care of in one day. My advice is to only look at what's in front of you. Take each detail one by one. If every detail cannot happen, remind yourself it's ok. The more you clear your mind of worries or thoughts that are not positive, the better you will see the light at the end of the detail road.

You are a mother with their lives in the palm of your hand. You are essentially the one in charge. What you say, think, and do will be modeled, practiced, and will become the truth in their world. Centering yourself is something that helps our brain understand this notion.

Purpose Becomes Clear

We may see ourselves becoming something that we weren't expecting. We may have seen ourselves becoming one thing but when we stop for a moment, we realize we are far from our goal. We have to remember that those goals and ideas were ours and not God's. He has our journey already mapped out. He already knows where we will be and who we will become. We simply need to give our goals to God and trust in the fact that our path will be paved in his glory.

Since I chose to stay at home, I gave up years of experience in my career of teaching. I had to be good with that decision. I knew if I stayed home, I was going to have a hard time getting back in the work force. That was exactly what happened. I was overlooked for teaching positions that went to others with more experience, but that was something I knew would happen. The fact that I was making several thousand less than a full time teacher would sneak up on me and I would have to learn how to reconnect to my purpose and not my wants.

A quote from Caroline Myss always helped me reconnect and center myself. She says, "The soul always knows what to do to heal itself. The challenge is to silence the mind." I always bring to mind this quote whenever I feel my ego try to control my purpose. Since I know working in the Learning Center at school with students having autism or below their grade level is my passion, I use this quote to bring me back to that joyous place.

Once I practice centering myself, breathing, noticing the space around me, and letting love and positive feelings come into my mind, my mindset changes. It seems very simple and it is. It really works.

As I begin to think about my job and what I do, I relate it to what the Universe wants me to do. What am I doing here? What does God have me doing? Am I here to help students who are not at grade level in math, reading, and writing as well as students who have social and behavioral difficulties? Does God have me working every day to touch a nerve in my students to help them learn and see themselves and the world around them a little differently? Absolutely! Once I find that within me, I use it each day in my morning routine. Remind yourself that you are here for God's plan, not yours.

Working with one student, I saw how much she was struggling with her own feelings. She needed to learn to feel them, get rid of the bad ones, and keep the good ones. She went from having meltdowns weekly, to once a month, and then once every three months. Ultimately, she was a student selected to give her promotion speech at her ceremony with the entire class and their parents. By me showing her how to deal with her emotions and by following my true passion, I showed the universe and myself how to move forward in my life.

Angel's Will Power

Because I saw her at least 2-3 times a week, I had the opportunity to talk to her. I found out where she moved from, her likes, and dislikes. When she would begin to have a meltdown, I would talk to her gently in order to calm her. If that didn't help, I took her outside the classroom door. I found that when I told her the truth about what her actions did to the others in the group, she was pulled back into reality. She didn't realize that her outbursts of anger were scaring the others.

One day during one of their 45 minute sessions, she immediately became upset and began crushing her glasses with her hands. Not saying a word, she was beginning to boil over. Because she sat between the two boys in our group, their eyes said it all. They became wide eyed boys with a look of fear. I asked her to walk outside in the hall with me. Next, I asked her to take a breath and exhale. I let her know that I didn't want to take away her feelings and make them unimportant, but I did let her know how her actions were altering the people around her.

When she heard that the boys, who were her favorite playmates at recess, looked frightened, her whole demeanor changed. She seemed to come out of the fog that was upsetting her. She began to realize that her friends were afraid of her and her behavior. She asked what she could do. As I told her they were fine, she seemed a bit relieved. Because she was so upset, she didn't realize her behavior lashed out on others. She was worried that the boys would be upset. I told her that everyone feels upset at one time or the other. I also reminded her that all she had to do was apologize for her actions and they would understand. By telling her these things, she let her own personality help her with her feelings and emotions.

As she apologized, she saw them return to themselves. She seemed to welcome that good news. When children lash out, they are not connected to their surroundings. Because they want to be accepted, they will try apologizes and behavior changes to get back to normal. Helping children through this helps create calm, peace, and models to them the steps to renewal.

Most students, who are not in control of their anger, are not trying to hurt those around them. It is the only way they know how to release the frustration built up. Since this is the way they've dealt with their anger, it has become a habit. The next step is to show them how to make a change. Modeling how to react to a frustration is the first thing. Then, remind them that they are in control of their own thoughts and feelings. Telling them that nothing is so bad as to warrant an outburst is a great resolution. Maybe no one has ever told the child about this logic. Finally, listening to what frustrates them is the most loving thing to show.

A Student's Story

Another student I worked with was in first grade. My job was to help him achieve his reading goal that was far below his classmates. Not only did he have to learn reading strategies, he had to begin to overcome his habit of crying when he didn't like the next step in his day.

Practicing transitions and giving him the tools to smoothly progress to the next lesson were set in place for him. However, I was trying to figure out a way for him to see the whole picture of school, so that he could see how he fit in.

In order to teach him how to move from hour to hour in his day, he was given a token board where he was able to move tokens from the back on Velcro to the front indicating that he was showing good behavior. This was a way for him to see his achievements right away and enjoy his accolades by receiving special rewards.

I always bring God into my daily life so this day was no different. I asked for guidance and an idea that I could use to help him receive an ah-ha moment. God put in my heart to introduce him to a 6th grade teacher just as we were walking from his classroom through the library where she was sitting. I introduced him to her.

He asked her a few questions and invited himself to her classroom. BAM! There it was! God was nudging me to use the visit to the upper grade as his reward if he practiced taking control of his feelings. With reminders each day for a week, he earned his visit the following week.

As we showed up to the sixth grade classroom as his reward, the teacher had already notified the students that he would be visiting and took his picture to display on the new monitor screen in their room. As the sixth graders came into class, they all greeted him with a high five or a wave and he sat with a student he was already friends from his neighborhood.

It was a time in their day where those students who completed all their assignments and work for the whole week could participate and enjoy their bonus P.E. outdoors. The others who did not complete an assignment or who forgot materials at home had to stay in class and complete their work. It was a good time to show him that even sixth graders were responsible for their actions and had to do their work. If they didn't complete it, they had to follow the rules and experience their consequence.

As some students left, I had him ask some of the upper graders why they were remaining in class. It was an eye opener for him as he realized that no matter whom you are, you have to follow school rules. He noticed they weren't crying or throwing a fit. They even expressed verbally to him what they did wrong to end up missing a fun event.

I asked them to tell him what they learned and what they would do differently. Some students choose to remain in the classroom to have fun on their laptops. He spent time circulating around the room asking questions and having conversations. Being such a young child, he was blessed with the courage he possessed of communicating with older individuals.

He helped the classroom teacher stamp their reflection sheets that they filled out by noticing what they achieved that week and what they had to work on for themselves. Being in first grade, he remembered that his class did the same thing. He stamped their paper after they read to him what they had written in their reflection.

As I sat back and monitored this first grader's interaction with these older students, it amazed me to see his wings begin to spread. It was exactly what he needed. When he returned to his first grade class, his teacher told me that he beamed the rest of the day. That was the answer from God for that day.

With God's help I simply asked for some guidance, I stepped out of my ego, listened to the answer, and acted upon it. When I stopped to dwell on why I wasn't a classroom teacher, my mind ceased to act upon the thoughts of why can't I get a better paying teaching job, and settled in with peaceful thoughts on how to help other individuals. I noticed someone needed help, I asked for help by praying, took the time to listen, and walked the student through the special moment he needed to help learn something about himself.

God's work is evident right at our fingertips. This was certainly an eye opener for me to realize that I may have dreams and thoughts of how I want to live. By following through with God's ideas and fulfilling God's work, we end up finding our real purpose.

Imagine if everyone everywhere did this on a daily basis? How much better would our lives be and the state of the world? Once we let go of the hold we have on a notion that isn't declared ours by God, we live in a more harmonious state. Every moment seems to have its exact reasoning. Every moment is unfolding for us to teach, learn, or enhance God's wisdom. This place we live in becomes calmer, more peaceful, and full of love.

Find Your Way

We are all here to find our purpose which is to help others in a way that is our own. Some people become firefighters, some pastors, some manage a food store, and some work retail, but within our daily lives of the work we do, we find our purpose in which to help, inspire, and lift up those around us.

No matter your calling, it will show up in what you learn and in how you demonstrate your work. Feeling stuck is something all parents will feel one time or another. It is the opposite of being unstuck. Think of a toy car that is controlled by a remote. The car can sometimes find itself lodged in a bush. For a time in which we choose, the car will remain there until we take action to free it from the bush.

Many of us feel the same way. We are stuck in the bush and we are not free because we have not taken the steps to do so. When we decide to dislodge our selves, then we are free. Some of us stay in the bush. Some of us do not decide to free ourselves for whatever reason. But it is ultimately our choice and we must be the one in charge of our freedom.

Sometimes we get stuck in the drama of our life and the small ridiculousness tugs on our ego. Move past the feeling of wanting to engage in the negativity. Return to that peaceful environment you practice creating. This is the Oneness you hear about. You are allowing everything to show its true self. Everything is connected. You begin to see how everything comes from one Source, Being, Divine. Be still so you can hear the advice of your guides, angels, or Divinity.

When you find it hard to get out of that funky feeling, change your thoughts to positive ones. At my tenth wedding anniversary, my goal was to visit Hawaii. As I sat on the beach of Maui, I looked out and marveled at the sight of whales breaching. I had my photo taken from the sandy beach as I sat in a lounge chair with me watching the wonderful sight of these wondrous whales. Upon returning from my peaceful stay in Hawaii to my hectic life as mother for an eight and five year old, I made sure to hang this photo on the refrigerator.

In those times of frustration with my children, I had this memory to visualize and relive. I would stop for a minute, breathe, and place my soul back on that beach. I recalled the whales breaching and sounds. It was a great way to revive myself. I could think clearer, focus on my task at hand, and eliminate the negative feelings.

As you venture down the wonderful road of infants, babies, and toddlers, remember to keep your heart opened and be ready to receive the best blessing. Keep your attitude bright toward your Source or God and be opened to the blessings that will come your way. You don't think our Divine will give us one of his wonderful souls without a plan to cover all their needs?

Even though I was a stay at home mom without a paycheck, I did not worry about money. It was as if my work of raising the girls was connected with my husband's salary. Because I kept in faith that I would receive everything needed and worked my tail off, I was blessed.

Live in the faith that you will do all things that you need to and your Divine or Source will take care of the rest.

Finding Our Soul's Connection

Our goal when raising our children should not be dictating over their thoughts, actions, and beliefs. Parents should remember to be guardians guiding their angels through their journey. With environments put in place that resemble what we see as energetic and loving, our children will feel safe and alive.

The Course of Miracles has been interpreted to state," Love is the intuitive knowledge of our hearts. Love isn't material. It's the feeling in a room, a situation, a person. It has nothing at all to do with the physical world, but it can be expressed nonetheless. We experience it as kindness, giving, mercy, compassion, peace, joy, acceptance, non-judgment, joining, and intimacy."

In response, our children will seek out the setting with the most comfort and feeling of peace for their life. Some souls live in an atmosphere where there is no kindness, love, and only negative aspects. But when they experience a climate of kindness, love, and generosity, our children's souls will meander toward that positive light.

Souls will seek the atmosphere that allows them to prosper and grow. We will recall that positive feeling and seek that hopeful surrounding. No one wants to live in a space of negativity, yet some souls do not realize that they have a choice not to do so. These precious souls, that are held hostage in an unloving arrangement, may not react or move toward the area of light until they experience the warmth love provides.

The best quote about souls comes from CS Lewis. He said, "You don't have a soul. You are a soul. You have a body." It is our job to create loving surroundings full of peace and joy for these souls we've created. We need to leave judgment out so our angels can flourish.

God isn't sitting around reliving and rehashing our wrong choices so why do we? Sometimes we may make a mistake in judgment when we raise our kids, but we need to remember to learn from it and move on. No more keeping score of our wrongdoings.

Chapter 6

Shift Your Intention to Guide & Transform

"Whatever opens us is never as important as what opens."

~Mark Neppo

As they say, there comes a time in all our lives when we feel a change coming on. Just when we are in the shift, we feel the urge to stop in order to hold on to what feels familiar. Not only do our children have many steps and stages to venture through, so do the parents.

It seems as though as soon as we are comfortable with one stage of development of our child, they shift into another and change takes place. We feel that we just mastered something we worked very hard to understand, and now that stage is ending and we are moving on to another stage. The mere word, change, can ruffle feathers.

Mark Nepo, a renowned poet and author, once said, "Whatever opens us is never as important as what opens." There will be places and things used in a particular stage that were needed then, but no longer serve us. It doesn't mean that those important aspects were not needed. It means they were no longer needed and it served its purpose. It was not only necessary but essential to understanding that particular stage in order to move on and grow.

A great example of this is the chrysalis of a butterfly. After the monarch sheds the enclosure and flies off to its next stage in life, its small chamber is what is left. It is no longer needed, yet it was the most essential piece in the stage at one point.

Transformation

We find many options needed for us to get through the stage we reside. Once we notice that a shift is occurring, we need to be happy in the fact that we had these helpful elements to use through our journey. Not everything is easy within each shift. Look for those blessings that helped you survive that stage. Be encouraged to find gratitude for having that wonderful stage of learning.

If the butterfly can move from a caterpillar to a flying insect, be reassured that our stages will have us shift and grow with changes put there for our good. We transform through many stages and levels using God's gifts. We need to realize that change is a good thing. Be aware that transforming is the way we move and grow through our journey.

Another example where learning takes place can be the example of a swimmer in the ocean. Sometimes you can be out in the sparkling water splashing about as if you have not a care in the world when suddenly you find yourself in a rip current. You begin to struggle and try to release yourself from the pull. You begin to pull hard through your stroke as panic takes over your nervous system. Harder strokes are probably the first thing we think to do when we find ourselves in that spot, yet the worst thing possible. When living a life near the beach, swimming with the current and not fighting it is always the first lesson of ocean swimming.

This is a lot like our own lives. If we would only stop and breathe, then venture off with the current and remain in faith, it will take us to a safe place. Since we are always on the move and believe that our way is the correct one, we never rely on the true One or God in charge. Sometimes, we have to take a leap of faith and trust in our own nature or God. It's a matter of practice. The more you give your trust, the more you live life without fear.

Think back to the time when we were youngsters. We didn't have a mortgage, car payment, or the need to appear as better than others. We did, in fact, have the knowledge that something else was in charge. If we take a moment to breathe in new situations that may feel uncomfortable, we can learn to rely on our Source or God and faith. In turn, let go of control and let what needs to happen occur.

As long as we put forth our best attitude, we can live freely in the knowledge that even though things are changing, we understand they need to happen. Live in the wisdom where only those things needing to occur will.

Be aware that our own thoughts can surely sour the positive attitude if we're not careful. Keep in mind what Wayne Dyer once said. "Keep reminding yourself: I get what I think about, whether I want it or not." If your thoughts veer off and attach to unfavorable ones, you are sure to have those come alive. Two things for a happy journey: Enjoying all simple aspects of life and letting the thoughts of others around you diminish and vanish.

If you think more decisively, your heart will resemble one with happiness. Happiness is a journey. In order to stay in the bliss of life, you learn it is something that has to be a conscious idea. If you want to be happy, you have to think that way. We can't be happy if our thoughts are negative. However, to help get rid of the negative thoughts, thank them for coming and let them move through your mind. Don't let them hang out and attach themselves by letting you relive them. A simple thank you for showing up, and then show them the door.

In order to preserve a positive attitude, Shawn Achor, the author of The Happiness Advantage stated, "Happiness is not the belief that we don't need to change. It's the realization that we can." In his book, he helps us learn, "Only 10% of your long-term happiness is predicted by your external world and circumstances. The other 90% comes from how you train your brain to process the world."

Be responsible for your own joy. Thich Nhat Hanh, a Vietnamese Buddhist monk and peace activist reminds us that, "The present moment is filled with joy and happiness. If you are attentive, you will see it." We cannot put the blame on someone else if we are not happy. A great way to accomplish this is to refrain from being offended. Our belief that someone is attacking us on purpose may be true, but by letting the insult drop and replace it with something positive, we turn our thoughts toward our own joy.

The more we learn to go with the flow, the more we will notice that we have more freedom and energy. We venture into our true bliss. We learn that with the simple knowledge of changing our mind's thoughts, we can remain in happiness. While we are learning to flow more and subside from going against the current in our lives, we are actually creating a stronger self.

Good Times, Bad Times

It is said that," Difficult roads often lead to beautiful destinations." Rest assured that you will encounter bad times and your children will go through some tough ones. It is your job as a parent to help guide them through it. So many parents want to take on the issue themselves in order to save their child from the pain.

Sometimes pain is good. It is good for your child to feel the pain of a mean friend, not completing their school projects in time, and receiving a failing grade. Allowing your child to feel the pain of their actions is necessary. If you continue to take on all their actions as your own, you are not creating a person who will someday be able to stand on their own.

What you want to do is help in a guiding manner. Think of yourself as a mentor. We are merely here as a parent to help instruct and be a tour guide for our student angels through the problem. Helping them become a problem solver for themselves is key to surviving in the world today.

A Daughter's Ah-ha Moment

There was a time back when my eldest daughter was just a few weeks into middle school. She was always an A student in elementary school and she could always seem to rely on her own study skills. Well, there it was, the day when she failed a math test at a 50%! After she hopped into the van at pick up time, she seemed to lose herself and her self worth. She wasn't one to show her emotions, so when she became a blubbering mess I knew this was big for her.

Uh oh, this is the onset of our stomach turning, our hearts sink for them, and we worry that this is the road to destruction leading to drugs and drinking. This is the time to put our intention into play. If we follow the ideas of breathing and flowing with the current of life, we will set ourselves up as parents to endure through the anxiety and anguish.

When you have children who are successful students in elementary school, it is good to keep in mind that the thought process changes as well as their expectancy to stay as a higher level thinker. As the parent, we are forced to stay out of their area, but seek a place at the sideline. Our children want to do things on their own and feel the freedom of doing them. But when they stumble, it is important to stay nearby, but not in their business until asked.

As spiritual beings, we tend to pray more in times of discomfort. Praying is a good practice, but so is learning to watch from afar. If we are smart, we will think back to our middle school days and remind ourselves that stuff happens. When it does, we need to let it happen, let them feel what happened, model peace, and stay calm. Let your angel know you are available to discuss it when they are ready. This is one of the hardest parts of being a parent, but the more you practice being a mentor and not a friend, the easier it gets.

She failed the math exam with a 50% and thought her life was to blame. Because she was the member on the local swim team, school volleyball team, and only accepted an A or higher as a score on any school work, she immediately started blaming all her activities and the difficulty of the course.

Since she felt that the other classes had too many goof offs and she had her eye on college, she wanted to be in the math honors course. FDR, our 32nd President of the U.S. once stated, "When you come to the end of your rope, tie a knot in it and hold on." The lesson she learned was hold onto the rope, calm yourself, and then practice to make a decision and start to climb back up.

In order to calm her grief, I suggested that she take a step back from everything she's doing and take a break from all activities until she felt better. I made sure I stated these things in a calm manner even though I was a bit nervous for her.

As she exclaimed that the math was so hard, I suggested that she move into the lower non-honors class for math to take the pressure off until next year. In addition, as an answer to her anguish from the many activities, I calmly suggested that she drop her activities and relax at home during the evenings completing her homework without pressure of a time constraint. The further we drove down the road, I could see the pressure leave her body. Wow, I thought, it really worked.

How Love & Communication Help the Process

When you realize that even in the middle of a storm you can react in a calm manner, you recognize the practice of going with the flow. You are taking the time to rely on your faith and let things happen. Truly, they happen for a reason.

Looking at the end result of her becoming a scholar collegiate swimmer, I see that the breakdown she suffered in middle school was supposed to happen. If I meddled in it and took control telling her what to do instead of letting her find it for herself, her college choice and situation could have gone very differently.

As she sat in the back of the van, she realized that it was only one test and her first ever fail. I asked her why she thought it happened. She felt that maybe she didn't really take it seriously and maybe she could have studied harder.

During this time of thought and going with the flow, she also realized that she had a love for the sport of swimming. She shared with me that while she swam her laps, she felt that it was a good way to feel peace similar to a meditation and a way to work out her stress of school.

It was an interesting time as a parent to experience her thought process. I was also let in on her likes and dislikes and why. When it came to volleyball, she mentioned that it was only for six weeks and then her time would open up to study more down the road.

All on her own, she ended up working out her problem because I allowed her to go with the flow. This was a moment in time that needed to occur. She had to realize what she could accomplish. It was important for her to feel the success of having a problem and using her thought process to figure it out. Being a parent who did not add to the upset, but offered a peaceful space to look for resolution, I learned the lesson of going with the flow and allowing my child to experience her own feelings.

Our drive was only about ten minutes, but probably the most important ten minutes of her life. Nonetheless, their problems may need to be slept on. It may take a few days to come to a conclusion. When our children go through these life stresses and problems, it actually helps them to grow inside. Her brain learned to seek refuge, find a peaceful quiet space to think, weigh all aspects, and then listen to her heart and follow its direction.

Teach Your Children Well

Bell Hooks, an American author, said, "Most children are amazing critical thinkers until we silence them." Think back to the time when your infant, who just learned to sit up, tried to put the square peg into the round hole. Remember how frustrated they became? Do you recall that when you let them alone to figure things out on their own they did things their way? They would try one way and then another.

We allowed them to explore and come up with different ideas to solve on their own as babies. We did this when they were trying to place an item in their mouth when eating. As parents we watched, but did not interfere. We didn't take their hand and put the item to their mouth for them. We let them accomplish that on their own. We knew that they would figure it out with practice.

As parents, we must do the same thing similar to our grade-schooler child when they try a harder math course or new sport. We have to let our child sort it out themselves. It is about learning to problem solve on their own. Coming up with ideas, trying them, noticing what didn't work, and coming up with another thought is the job of our child, not the job of a parent.

Think back to the time when our little angel was sitting at the high-chair and trying to figure out how to pick up the circled cereal and put them in their mouth? That was their lesson that day. We were probably busy putting dinner in a crock pot or placing dishes into the dishwasher than watching and interfering.

Moment by moment, our angel kept trying to maneuver their tiny chubby fingers around the cereal piece. We weren't interfering in every try as they used their hand or spoon to reach their mouth.

Recall the earlier times when your angel was learning new lessons. In the process of our angel's eating exercise, we stayed out of the moment and permitted the task to take place. As they practiced crawling, walking, or riding a bike for the first time, we let them use all their own ideas to work it out. We didn't move their knees for them when practicing to crawl. We sat nearby and cheered for them. As they took those first few steps, we smiled and held our arms out saying encouraging words. When they took off on their bikes after falling a half dozen times, we were there shouting supportive words and clapped until our hands hurt.

So why would you take over for them while they are in the midst of their new lessons? We have to let them forget their project or book report, fail a test they didn't study for, and let them live the consequences that come with their actions. Allow them to receive the poor grade. Sit by and let them figure out their next step. Let them forget their homework and go to detention. Be there to pick them up afterwards asking if they learned their lesson rather than fight with the teacher about attending all together.

Do exactly what you would do as they learned to ride their bike. Be a parent and have wound spray with band aids handy for all their scrapped knees during the bike falls in life. Let them feel the pain of the consequences. Don't take them on for them; otherwise they don't learn that lesson.

We lived our lives and made our mistakes. It's time to let our children live theirs. Just be there to guide and not do for them. Once you let them do things for themselves, you are one step closer to watching them pack to travel the world on their own.

Second Daughter's Realization

Fear can stop anyone in their tracks and sway us from our intention. It's the unknown. It's scary and it can mess up our expectations. Be the parent who notices the lesson inside our child's fear.

As she ventured into the sport of volleyball, my younger daughter, who loved volleyball, learned how certain positives came with negatives. Volleyball is a big sport in southern California. If you had skills, the right coach could make you shine. The right coach can also teach you some real world experiences to help you on your path.

Volleyball teams are formed at a young age. While sitting in the stands of her sister's middle school volleyball games as a fifth and sixth grader, Tara realized her love of the game. With her long legs and long fingers, she knew her body was made for the sport. When it was her turn to tryout, she made the middle school team easily.

Her first lesson was learning that the coach's children always play before others no matter their skills. Since her fingers were long and nimble, her coach (who turned out to be an Olympic Gold medalist) noticed and helped her understand the setter position. Because it's hard to run a team on your own, he had an assistant.

The assistant coach had a daughter on the team who also enjoyed playing the same position. So whenever the head coach wasn't at the weekend games, the assistant coach never let my daughter play setter. She knew she had the skills because her coach always validated her by telling her. At a specific game, she had to step into her greatness and walk up to her fear meeting it head on.

As she figured out that she would not get to play, after attending all the practices the week before and seeing that her team would win the match in a few points, she felt it all boil to the surface. At the age of eleven, she had her first bout with her fear.

While standing on the side line, her disappointment showed on her face. Once again, she was overlooked and didn't get to play. The team had one more match to play, but since her expectations were shattered, she turned to me and said she wanted to quit as she walked out of the complex. I followed her to the van and we sat and talked. First, she cried and let all her frustration out. Next, she stated why she was upset and became adamant about not returning. At that point I thought, "Ok, its show time, Mom."

Use Love, Connect & Be Present

The first thing I did was make sure that she let all her resentment out of her mind. After the crying subsided, I began to have her look at her future in volleyball as well as life without it. By doing this, I asked what she liked about volleyball. As she started looking at the positive side of it, her face lit up while she listed all the things she loved about the game.

After that, I tried to show her what the future might hold for her. I reminded her there will be many more times where she will be on the sideline and this was practice for life. If she was smart, she wouldn't take it personally, but use it as a tool to learn the true meaning of endurance. Be a parent who steps back allowing them to learn how to sustain and tolerate certain things that might not feel good, and persevere.

Along with the realization that play time cannot be guaranteed, I had her visualize herself trying out in older level club teams. With that, she did the same in her mind for high school volleyball. The most important thing I left her with was the fact that she was given a gift, yet she wasn't sure what it was going to be used for. I reminded her to remember that every practice and game was there for her to learn something. She was also given the gift to enjoy.

Digging Deep Inside

I told her briefly the stories of Michael Jordan and Shaquille O'Neal. As she began to listen to how these powerhouses started off sidelined and benched, her heart opened up to the fact that it wasn't all about playing every game. Reminding her that not all children get to play a sport made a big jolt in her mind.

This grounded her and brought her down to reality. It was about using her gift, doing her very best, and one day using this gift to serve someone else. It wasn't about being the star every moment. She also had a chance to notice her grit. Having sportsmanship was the most important thing to learn and show up at every practice and game. Being the one shining your light to help others find their way was our theme.

During the visualization, it came up that she may be a great player that spends time on the sideline. If she wanted to play, she would have to feel these disappointments, lower her expectations, learn as much from that view, and be the best cheerleader for the rest of the team.

Now looking at her accomplishments from age eleven through college, her lesson learned at eleven was her turning point. She can trace the beginning of her journey in volleyball from that decision she made at the age of eleven in her purple van. She decided to do her best and stay with it because she loved the sport and wanted to learn all she could.

Although she turned out to have great success on her club teams and being selected to play on a national team, she only made the high school team one year. Every summer she would prepare for high school tryouts, and every year she found herself the last one cut. But if you ask her now what she learned from that entire ordeal, she learned her true strength.

Realization of a Scholar Athlete

With all the work she put into her club season, she was selected as the top recruited player for her university. Since you need to tell a brief story on your college application showing a time when you learned your strength, she had her experience to fall back on. Filling out those applications and writing those essays, she realized that standing on the sideline all those years ago helped her find her future college.

We all have these circumstances that will put us face to face with our fear. How we're going to handle it is up to us. We can either be the obnoxious athlete who only cares about herself, or we can stay grounded in how can we serve others with our gifts.

She found the true meaning of her volleyball gift. She was excited to play as an incoming college freshman, which is rare, but had to dig deep inside and remind herself how to be strong when she was faced with a bruised femur and missing many games as a junior and senior. Being three thousand miles away from home didn't help. Yet through it all, she would do it all over again.

Her realization became clear to her as she worked during the summer of junior college year. As an intern at her volleyball club organization, she worked updating the profiles of the players and was asked to fill in and coach for a young girl's team. There it was. Her gift was to learn the game, endure waiting to play, and suffer injuries so that she could one day share her experiences with younger girls who one day want to play for a university.

When we look back at the trail of popcorn we leave behind, we can see where we came from and what we endured. If we're smart, we pack it all up as souvenirs to pass along to the next ones who walk down our similar path. It is all about creating our intentions in anything we are involved in. Acknowledge circumstances that are not the ones you dreamed up, all the while finding the qualities that you can use to serve others.

It truly is about learning to weather the storm with your intentions. One day if we look closely, we will see what our endurance and intentions do for us. After her internship and graduation from college, she was offered a volunteer volleyball coaching experience through her church during their mission to Hungary.

It is amazing what God shows us if we walk up to our fear, acknowledge it, and kindly walk past it. We are shown why we were given our gifts in the first place. She had the honor of coaching youngsters with tough circumstances. She shared her stories of how she found her strength through her volleyball experience. Through those two weeks in Hungary, she realized her intentions helped her serve others who may one day need to go face to face with their fear.

Chapter 7

Fear vs. Love

"Love is what we were born with. Fear is what we learned here."

~**Marianne Williamson**

Motherhood comes with the emotions of love one moment, but then the feeling of fear the next. As a part of the human experience, we are taught to stay away from fear and all aspects of it. In fact, we should actually hold hands with our fear. Steven Pressman, an American author of historical fiction, non-fiction, and screenplays, refers to this fear as Resistance with a capital letter.

He has taught me that when fear comes up in our life, it is our angels calling us to go up to a higher level. As we have continued to defeat our fears from past events, we are rewarded by being lifted higher toward our true self and peaceful oneness. If we do not realize this, we can begin to struggle with self sabotage and only focus on fear and the idea that something is wrong with us.

As a scholar athlete, this is one of the hardest things to do; keeping a positive mind free from fear is a daily challenge. Since these students are constantly fighting the fear of being good enough, here are some ideas that can help a mom strengthen their child's mind to use loving strategies to replace fear-based ones.

Choose Love to Overcome Negativity

The form that fear takes on is found in our negative thoughts. As we let the emotions of fear take effect, we begin to panic and try to react to demolish it. Instead, our reaction toward fear should be to recognize that it is a sign we are moving up a level of our spirituality. Because we are practicing different forms of meditation such as finding quiet places for peace, learning to connect with our own voice, and learning the importance of welcoming positive thoughts over negative ones, we are approaching a time in our life of growth. As we progress toward our best selves, we are confronted with fear. Hitting fear head on with love is the answer.

Matt Kahn, a spiritual teacher and author, has taught me that fear should never be something that we just drop, move aside, or push down into our stomachs in order to get away from it. On the other hand, fear should be treated like an infant. At a meet and greet with Matt, he replied to my worry about fear of writing and taking on my book. "Would you just drop and leave a baby?" He asked. "Of course not," I blurted out.

No one would act that way, but that is the way many of us treat fear. We see it as a negative thing, whereas it is actually there to help us move forward. Matt reminded me to acknowledge the fear, remember to love it and myself, and be ok in its presence.

Only allow that which is good to enter your life. Push fear with the love of a smile. Push fear back by your smile. Smile as the fear is replaced by love. Being consistent in allowing love to conquer the fear is key as a parent. When issues come up with our children, right away we start to think that we are the problem, we are not good enough, and we are weak. It is very easy to seep into that negative place, but by counteracting fear with the presence of love, we realize that this fear is here for a reason. We need to push through the fear like we are walking through a turnstile.

With all of our powerful thoughts, we must grant ourselves permission to stand strong by seeing ourselves as positive creatures trying to move past this particular lesson and our dream, destiny, and purpose. Fear is only the opposite of love. Meditate through the false ideas moving through your head and replace them with the knowledge that you can defeat fear. The more you defeat the fear in your mind, the closer you get to realize your dream.

Facing Fear Head-on

This fear comes in many forms. It could be the people you surround yourself with, the unfavorable reflections about others in a judgmental way, or the feelings of unworthy or incapable of being a good parent. Jack Canfield stated, "Everything you want is on the other side of fear." We have to make up our minds and decide whether we want to achieve our goal and dream or let it vanish. Remember, when fear enters our lives, we can look at it in a positive way. This is a time that our angels are calling us to go up higher.

Racing from school events, birthday parties, and family functions, our daybook becomes limited and provides time for fear to make its appearance. As soon as our children meet head on to a stress in their lives, we seem to take it on as our own. The stress that we feel is our worry that they may withdraw and reject us as their parent. This is the time to take Wayne Dyer's words and meditate on love. He expressed, "You cannot always control what goes on outside. But you can always control what goes on inside."

This is a great time to use communication skills. Outlining what your child feels is the problem will help alleviate their stress. Offering the lighter side of circumstances helps them see that others can certainly have bigger troubles. Creating peace and quiet at this time is essential. Eliminating devices at this time helps the environment fill with positive thoughts and love.

Understand that life will throw many circumstances that look like problems at you and your child, but by taking Wayne's words to heart, you will be able to press through the fear of the problem and find the lesson. We are parents trying to keep all harm from our children. However, a parent doesn't realize that all the fear and problems that come at us are there to help us grow while our children are growing. Those of us in the empty nest stage have the look on our face of, "Oh, now I understand why that happened."

As a parent, we know all too well that when our children are in pain, so are we. Their pain may be coming from a failed test, failed relationship, unrealized expectations, or manipulations from people they trusted. When any of these happen, we want to jump right in and help. We've lived through these disappointments and feel we know the answer.

Be sure to promote yourself as an ear to listen to the problem rather than the loud mouth of a lecturer. Give out opinions and advice when they ask. By blurting out your circumstance and the solution that helped you, they may not be in a place to hear it.

When they solicit your advice, it is because they have already felt the feelings, mulled it over in their mind, and are now ready to hear options to help them move through the situation. If you look back at your own life, you probably looked to your friends when needing advice. Avoid letting your negative thoughts create the false talk that you are being rejected when your children go to their friends. Show peace by behaving calm around the child who is experiencing stress.

Adding the stress of a pushy parent is not the answer. Helping to create and maintain a sense of peace in the home will help your child work out the grievance in their time. This is an important time where you as a parent have to be the mentor. It is your time to take center stage in your life and become the best example of yourself for your child.

Keep in mind what Wayne Dyer once said, "Remind yourself that you cannot fail at being yourself." Let love remain on your mind. Pray positively that everything happens in order to learn a lesson. Pray that your child will learn the lesson on their own. Pray that your love is around and present for them. Pray love and not fear.

Fear Nothing

If we think about it, fear is the hardest road block, yet the simple path to take to achieve and realize our dream and destiny. Any form of meditation that fits you helps the voices fade allowing only the answer to become clear. God is right there with you. By avoiding the fear, you will not move closer to your dream. Know that your Divine Source will continue to give you many chances to overcome this particular fear. You will see it come up many times. Get to the point in your mind that fear can be overcome and as Nike says, "Just do it!"

When feeling lost, defeated, and alone, now is the time to practice your meditation. Start by reminding yourself that you are worth the pit stop. Your life deserves the best medicine. Find your quiet place. Sit and give yourself permission to come to a halt. Experience the moment you are in by looking around your home and noticing the fish tank motor, the rustling of the leaves and branches on the trees outdoors, and your own breathing. Over power the negative thoughts with life. Allow only positive thoughts to enter your mind. Be strict in this process. Slow down, unwind, and calm yourself are the key goals. Find your peace. Notice the best things in your life.

Even more, you're giving this process as a gift to your family because they watch you, they learn, and notice this way of life. They notice the calm and experience the peace right along with you. They learn by doing it themselves. You have just become a positive example to your family. This is your gift of your presence.

Your Presence of Love as Your Gift

Strolling through the first five years of my children's lives, I knew how important those precious years can be in the development of their brains. Because of this knowledge, my daily rituals and activities matched what my children's brains needed to grow.

I lived by Wayne Dyer's famous quote, "Our intention creates our reality." Since my intention was to teach and learn at least one thing each day when I was home with them, I scheduled and consistently arranged daily activities so to nurture and educate my girls in some way.

As I scheduled library trips, math and letter writing time, and games, it was important to me to live in that moment. I worked hard to eliminate any worry or thought that wasn't involved in what I was doing. Daily travels in and out of the car can be a lot of work when children are young. Allowing your children to pull out their puzzles and toys can leave you with the burden of cleanup.

Try to keep in mind that all of these moments have an ending. When your children grow up and enter the higher grade levels of elementary school, they will no longer be breaking out their many toys like a child does when they are younger. Feeding them at their high chair and even sitting at the edge of the bathtub will soon be a memory.

When mothers mention that their children grow up at the snap of a finger, it is very true. One minute you are collecting the toys and books when it's their nap time and before you know it, they will be on their phone with their door shut to the outside world chatting with friends.

A way I kept in the moment was creating my own photo books. By using a composition book, I had photos developed and then spent their nap times taping them in the notebook. (Back in the day before Smartphones with cameras.) I spent time writing small paragraphs about where we were in the pictures.

I'm aware that the times were different, but it is still easy to send some of your pictures taken on your phone and set up a photo developing system through CVS or another company offering this option. Most pictures went into photo albums, but it was fun to select a few and write about my memory of that special day. There are also new ways of creating photo books to visually look at online. Either way, collect the memories and let them add to your happiness.

Before long, they were becoming teenagers. Since I stored these under my bed, I came across them as I cleaned. It was so fun to give my daughters these special handmade photo albums now that they were older. I waited until summer so they could take time to look at them. They would spend time giggling on the couch together sharing their books with each other. As they read the captions, I could hear their excitement of reliving the past.

Making Memories

One of my best memories was when I spent a few hours in the fall with my girls chasing a Dollar Store kite up and down the sandy beach. Talk about simple. I probably had a dollar in change and picked up a kite from one or those ninety nine cent stores while the girls were in school. After I picked them up, I handed them some baggies of snacks of pretzels and banana bread slices and told them we were going to have a surprise. We headed to the beach on a roundabout way. I took them to a beach that we didn't frequent much to make the experience a little different. As we got there, I grabbed the bag that the kite was in and headed to the beach. I could hear them mumbling to themselves asking what's up.

I reached into the bag and pulled out the kite. The look on their faces let me know that it was purchased for a dollar and looked it. I could feel their disappointment but I didn't let on. I laid the kite in the sand and started letting out the string. I stopped to feel which way the wind was blowing, smiled at them with a wink, and started running down the beach. Because it was a windy day, it took no time to ascend with the seagulls.

Only after a few times up and down the beach the girls ran over wanting to have a turn. Each took turns holding the string and maneuvering the kite to play off the wind. All you could hear was laughing and giggling. That went on for a good hour and I made sure I took pictures with a throw away camera. (This was before the Smartphone selfie craze.)

When it was time to go do homework and make dinner, the van had a great vibe. During the sound of huffing and puffing, I could still see their smiles and heard the banter of who had the kite the highest. That was a great memory. We were definitely living in the moment.

The more we strive to live in the present moment, the more we will get out of life. The author of The Power of Now, Echart Tolle, mentions, "Realize deeply that the present moment is all you ever have." Once we grasp this notion, we begin to live a more meaningful life.

Great Minds Have Purpose

While you incorporate activities to help you live in the present moment, look into video that can help all be present. You may notice that your child doesn't seem to pay attention very well to parents, teachers, or others. They actually struggle to live in their moment. It is true that some children can't pay attention because their brain hasn't finished developing.

For instance, if a child begins to crawl earlier than expected or walk before their first birthday, their brain can become incomplete in areas that will show up later in language development or reading. When these highways in the brain are not fully developed, our child may find themselves struggling in everyday functions.

By looking into the vestibular and proprioceptive systems of the brain, parents can learn and understand what is needed to help their child become fully functioning individuals.

The founder of Brain Highways, Nancy Green, has wonderful videos, a Ted Talk, and programs to help your child achieve their development and goals. While medication can sometimes be needed for our child, I believe that the first step to develop our children's brain is through researched based programs. If you go to her website or look up other videos and information about the vestibular and proprioceptive systems, you will gain knowledge about how these systems, if not properly working, can hold back your child's learning.

It is known that with problems in the midbrain areas, students' actions can look similar to symptoms of ADD and/or ADHD. Some of these problems may show up in school subjects of reading as well as comprehension of text. Arming yourself with information and videos will help your child move closer to living their true life.

Since parents can also have underdeveloped brains, videos found online would be a great help and warrant parents spending quality time with their child. Live in the moment, practice being still during your time with your angels, and enjoy them that very minute.

Whether you stay at home full time or work, the life of a mother is never ending. Trying to find time to live in the moment during these hectic times can be a struggle. Taking time to create these memory books or play a game with your child should be your goal. It is a way to live in the now.

Dr. Jon Kabat-Zinn, the creator of the Center of Mindfulness in Medicine, believes, "You can't stop the waves, but you can learn how to surf." Being brave enough to educate yourself and your child is the most valuable gift along with your presence and love that you can offer to your child.

Keep Conversation Alive

Knowing that your presence and love are so powerful, one can infer that speaking out loud to your child can do the same thing. It saddens me to see young mothers either texting or fiddling on their phone as they walk their child in a stroller. Yes, sometimes there are important matters that must be handled immediately, but this is an area where scheduling comes into play. Create time to spend precious moments connecting with your child by speaking to them when strolling. Carving out these special moments of time will be very noticeable when it comes to their reading and language development.

As I taught, I came across this statistic: Children retain only 10% of what they read, 20% of what they hear, but they retain 90% of what they say and do. When you are walking, be sure to look around and comment on the things around you like the flowers, the clouds, and the smells in the air and direct your conversation to your child.

Ask your child about what they see and then have them use whatever adjectives they can think of when describing. Add words to their adjective list by speaking them aloud. Engage in interactive conversation with your little one. Even if they aren't speaking yet, put your attention on them. As a mom of two college students, you can never get back those precious moments. Take the time to live in the now and actually schedule time to be off your phone.

During their elementary and middle school years, connect with your children with a trip to the outdoor mall. Treat them to fresh lemonade and a peek at the windows with the new fashions. Direct all your questions towards their feelings on the colors and their opinion about an outfit during window shopping. Put on your listening cap and get ready to learn new things about your child through their own words.

While beginning high school, one daughter wanted to color the tips of your hair a bright pink color. Now days, non-permanent hair color is available, so sit them down and take advantage of them being in one place. Ask them open ended questions like," What is your favorite class? Have you met any new friends? What do you like about them?" This is the perfect time to find out what they are thinking, what some of their likes and dislikes are, and why.

Connecting and communicating during the college years is a breeze thanks to the new technology. I can send a quick good morning and good night text to show my love. Because we set as a rule in our family that a quick answer was needed for all texts, we receive confirmation that they are doing ok with a little hello.

Face Time, Skype, and Zoom are wonderful ways to feel like your child is right there when they're in their dorm. These help remove the fear in your heart about how they're doing. You get to check on their physical and spiritual health with just a glimpse. I have learned to keep both texting and video chats brief. Let the amount of time be determined by them. This will guarantee them seeking you out instead of the parent becoming the dreadful helicopter mom. In turn, your fear will be replaced with their love as they connect with you.

Chapter 8

Nurture Your Children without Control

"It is our obligation to guide our angels and help them discover their aspirations that are meaningful to them."

~P Kellenbarger

One of the most important ideas to remember is when we raise or rear our children; we must remember that we are acting as their guide, monitoring their actions in order to help keep them safe and secure. When you begin utilizing these four keys of love, schedule, communication, and consistency, be aware that as a parent, we help pilot our angels toward their journey.

We need to keep in mind that they need to reach for their dreams, passions, and interests. If our children want to advance their education by attending college, it is our job to help them toward that goal. If our children are excited about playing different sports, we should help guide them by giving them our support and love. Being aware of our own feelings on these subjects is essential. It is our obligation to guide our angels and help them discover their aspirations that are meaningful to them.

It is known that some parents want to raise mini-me's, which are children that they control and maneuver to fit and finish living their own dreams. Keeping our wants and needs out of the hands of our children is one of our most important tasks.

Yes, it would have been wonderful for both my husband and I to watch our children run track and play soccer, but those were not their interests. Because they enjoyed individual sports being that they lived near the beach and loved to surf, we signed them up at the local YMCA with the swim team for three months.

Guiding & Pulling Back Control

Being strong swimmers, this would only help them with their surfing and was the only time we signed them up for any sport. This was also when they were fairly young at the ages of eight and ten. We wanted them to experience an individual sport where they would also meet other children.

At the onset of this enlistment, we told them up front that it was only for three months and that we wanted them to experience being on a team. They were aware that after the three months, they didn't have to continue and there would be no argument. It turned out that our youngest made it to the Junior Olympics with her freestyle team, but found that volleyball was more her taste. Our eldest ended up swimming for her college for four years and qualifying each year to the MAC Swim Championships back east.

Keep in mind, we did sign them up for swim since it was connected to their likes and would help with their love of surfing, but we also let our children have control of their interests after that experience. Purely for educational purposes, we were parents that signed our children up for a sport. We wanted them to experience a team sport and get a feel for what that might be for them.

Tour Guide

In your children's lives, arrange to have them try new things for the exposure and to experience a feel for what's out in the world. Letting them decide whether it is for them should be their decision.

Parents are guides through this place we call life. We have to teach manners and daily decorum, as well as teach them the rewards and consequences for their actions. Letting them decide on what activity they want to do should come from them. We are merely here to help them venture off toward their road. We need to let them have their interests, imagination, and choices. Having children to relive your glory days is a poor decision. That will only alienate them and create a distance between parent and child.

Our main job is to let our angels find their own passions and explore them. Our job is to help them realize that they should try to harness it if that is what they want. No one is at their pivotal best when they begin their families. We are constantly working on becoming our best selves.

While you teach your children behavior, continue to work on yourself in front of them. Do this by sharing your new list of ways to show more love with them that you hung on your mirror. Share the new authors who help you find your inner peace and the ways you are following to be successful. Find some quiet time and read some pages that interest you that may motivate them. Give them the best example of one who can seek wisdom.

In the past, they have commented on the sheet of quotes I taped to the bathroom mirror. I did it more for myself, but I was happy to hear that they were reading them too. I've also passed them names and videos of people who have struck a chord with me. I always present them by saying this video helped me think differently. It's best to present ideas to them without any strings attached. Be sure not to take anything personally either. If they aren't touched by the person who brought you so much help, let them move on and find someone that touches their soul.

Gretchen Rubin, author of *Happiness Project*, stated that, "When we change our habits, we change our lives." While we are moving through each day of our lives as parents, we should not regret feeling insecure or uncomfortable.

As we feel scared or anxious, it is a fact that as we change these feelings, we will be moving in a positive direction. It is necessary to move forward, so as we learn strategies to turn our insecurities into peaceful composure, we grow as individuals and show our metamorphosis.

Free Your Child from Your Control

One of the hardest things to let go, as a mother, is control of your child. Control, meaning having restraint or direction over something or someone, is a small part of motherhood that does take place in order for us to teach. It is one of the difficult challenges because we have to control some aspects around our daily lives with them.

The secret to letting go of the control over our children is to control our own actions. It is said from Tao Te Ching, "The hard and stiff will be broken. The soft and supple will prevail." We must slowly and silently withdraw from the surveillance over their actions and at the same time let them come into their own nature.

For instance, teaching them how to hold their spoon and cup happens in the early years. We use command words when we help them find direction. In a way, we regulate and guide them when they are in our presence. We are constantly guiding them away from harm and into safety.

As they try their hardest to use their spoon to pick up a mouthful, we are using our words and actions to model the best form. We move from this mastery to controlling what they see and do. Regulating what our child view online or on television is a big task in itself.

During the elementary years, we may have more regulation in the form of reminders such as staying off the table and chairs, keeping hands to ourselves instead of on our siblings and friends, and following up on their chores and homework. These limitations are helping our children learn and practice completing their responsibilities.

This controlling by guiding and regulating goes on through all stages of their developing and helps in the aging process of our own hair color as parents. Remembering that as parents, we don't know everything. It is not a weakness to let your children know this. At the same time, understand that it is a way of showing your love. It may help your child to see you as a truthful person who is looking out for their good. They will always see you as the authority, but sometimes it reminds them that parents are human and make mistakes just like them.

Controlling is the way a parent acts upon their child after the rules have been taught and laid down. Controlling takes place when the parent continues to interfere. We have all read or seen a movie where the controlling mother is constantly spitting on the hanky to clean the son's face or fixing and fumbling with the son's hair while he is an adult. It is important to put a restriction on yourself when it comes to letting go of the actions of your child.

For instance, when my daughter was playing high school and club volleyball, there was a mother who always had to be within two feet of her daughter with water, handing off team shirts, or trying to join in the team conversations after a match. As a mom watching this spectacle, a feeling of embarrassment came over all parents sitting and waiting for their daughters. Of course we want to be right there in the conversations too, but that is for the players, not the parents. Be aware of your actions and if you find yourself behaving like this, cut the cord and maybe practice waiting in the car after a game.

As a spiritual person, I never wanted to suffocate the imagination or free thinking of my childrens' minds. Yet, I was not a believer of letting my children rule the roost. Children need to know that they can think and act freely, but under a small amount of guidance.

Letting Them Take Control

At the age of four, my daughter wanted to attend a Memorial Day ceremony at a cemetery where a murdered victim from the past laid to rest. A woman was staying at the Hotel Coronado back in the late 1800's when she died under mysterious circumstances. Since my daughter loved ghosts, skeletons, and cemeteries, we read the book together and attended the service. She was a girl who wore all pink at one point, but then transitioned to black with skulls.

What I'm trying to advise is to let your angel go in the direction that they were put on this earth to follow. Nurture their interests, learn new things yourself, and watch them spread their own wings while helping you extend and stretch yours.

This daughter of mine ended up finding one of the best colleges in the nation to learn about archaeology. She studied at Lycoming College in Pennsylvania which has the most renowned professors in the areas of archaeology and art history. She found a significant wall area while on one of her archaeological digs in Cyprus. After graduating with two majors and two minors, her next step was graduate school at Temple University to receive her PhD. When you let go of the control over your child's every thought, they simply align with their path and begin to follow that energy.

While she attended Lycoming, one of her dreams came true when she took place in an archaeological dig in Cyprus. Even during the horrible threat of IsIs in the Middle East, she packed her bags and went toward her adventure. Understand that my spiritual practice of praying and meditating took over my brain those eight weeks, and brought me closer to myself and the oneness I seek. Wearing cut off tee shirts, minimal makeup, and doing her laundry in a bucket, she lived her life on her terms traveling down the road of her journey because her parents dared to release the control over her.

Again, letting go is one of the most terrifying yet most rewarding steps to take when you are raising your children. Keep in mind that taking small steps is the best way to practice releasing control while they venture through the elementary and adolescent years. As you let go of the small things, this will allow you to do so when the bigger obstacles come along during the high school and college years.

Now don't get me wrong, when it comes time for dating and driving, we can relax the control by using set rules. This gives them the guidelines with the freedom of making their choices.

If we didn't let our daughter make her choice of continuing her swimming, she would not have become the great scholar athlete that she became. If we took charge of her life and controlled her studying, sports, and time at home when she became overwhelmed by her failing grade, she would have never felt the accomplishment of going through a stressful time and coming out the other end victoriously. If we never helped her seek her interests, she would have never sat in her ditch in Cyprus and never would have located an important find.

When we free our children from our control, they learn to rely on their nature, their intuition, and their thought process. They learn to be confident in their own skin. Taking the control off your children helps them realize and become the person they're supposed to be.

Eliminate Shame from Your House

When we eliminate shame in our home, we create children who use guilt talk and not shame talk. When we teach our children to stand up for their feelings by using self talk, it reminds them that they didn't deserve a certain treatment. They are not shaming themselves, but feeling the humiliation. For example, when my oldest daughter came home from school in the third grade, she brought up at dinner the fact that she had a sub who humiliated her. When we asked her what happened, she said the sub was using a strategy for writing letters in the air, but she told all lefthanders to sit down and not participate. The substitute teacher was leaving out students because her knowledge was lacking.

My daughter said she was so mad at that sub. She called her a jerk and mentioned she didn't deserve that. How dare she do that to the lefties of the class? My daughter could have said, "Oh no, what did I do to deserve this? I'm so dumb as a leftie." Right there, I realized that she felt humiliated and I couldn't save her from that, however I saw how she saved herself by her own self talk. She didn't put herself down for the situation that the substitute created.

When we create a home environment that squashes any bullying remarks between siblings, we are creating individuals that will stand up for them self. By stating that your children are awesome, but their behavior is what needs to change, than you are creating minds that will avoid addictive behaviors, getting involved with drugs, promiscuous sexual behavior, and depression. Raising your child to notice that their behavior is bad and not them is key.

A few years later in middle school, she showed her quality of being a procrastinator. Her project and paper were due the next day and it took students 5 days to complete. Not my daughter. She did the writing on her own and completed the doll, with a little help from her parents, and received a B. When I called her a procrastinator, she was quick to tell me that she wasn't a procrastinator, but maybe has the qualities of one. She finished by telling me she works the same way as a diamond, because beautiful things are created under pressure.

I remember chuckling at that, however now I'm in awe of her ability to see herself for whom she really is.

Her young sister was increasingly becoming self made as well. Maybe it was hearing how her older sister talked, and maybe it was also by the way she was raised with specific rules that avoided putting someone in shame. Because they grew up knowing that was not accepted, they were able to experience guilt, humiliation, and embarrassment. They experienced these feelings by looking at their behavior and not connecting it to themselves by negative self talk.

Using words like, "your choice of behavior wasn't a good one," or, "You are an intelligent person, so you should work on how you are making others feel when you speak to them that way," are good phrases to practice when speaking to your child. As parents, we need to understand how powerful words are and notice it when we speak to our kids. We want to avoid any kind of shaming so that they avoid negative self talk about themselves.

Because of raising my daughters by not tolerating any kind of shaming and putting my foot down, I believe it's the reason for their success in their short lives. They were scholar athletes all through high school and undergrad college years. Since they didn't put themselves down, they always had their own cheering section right inside of them.

Chapter 9

Be Friendly, Not Their Friend

"Please be responsible for the energy you bring into this space."

~Dr. Jill Bolte Taylor

There will be battles to pick and battles to let fall by the waist side. Be sure that if you have a competitive side along with being stubborn, your little angel has the same features. Being friendly and not their friend, you are setting up the proper hierarchy as parent and child by creating secure rewards and consequences. This chapter will also help you understand what they really are and how to use them best.

As you review your morals and beliefs and decide what you want in your household, be sure to stick to them with all the consistency you can muscle up. Alongside consistency, love must exist in order for learning to take place. Following these strategies sets up your little angels to becoming coachable individuals which is needed to become a successful scholar athlete.

Wayne Dyer had a way of reminding us to keep our hearts opened by remaining in love, staying connected to our Source, and reminding us to see the goodness in everyone no matter their circumstance or behavior. "You are a creature of Divine Love connected at all times to Source. Divine Love is when you see God in everyone and everything you encounter." Dyer's quote is a wonderful reminder that any actions of our children are just that. They are actions that we experience, but should never attack with anger. Removing ourselves or the child while our ninety seconds of turmoil runs its course is the smart move.

For example, if it is important to you that your child uses their manners when receiving a gift or item, make it clear to your offspring that gratitude is something your family practices. There may be a situation when your child refuses to acknowledge it. As they flex their muscles, be sure to approach it in a kind way. Remind the child that a thank you is in order.

If you are willing to take the time to enforce your rule at that moment, be ready to wait it out. Some of our angels have the same wonderful temperament as we do and will hold out as long as possible. By doing the waiting game, be sure to be consistent in all your actions. Remind your child that this is a belief that will be followed and ignoring it will lead to a consequence.

Ruling with a Peaceful Fist

Remaining calm in an environment of peace is the best manner to model family rules. In a pleasant and consistent manner, let the child know that the rule of gratitude will be followed and not ignored. By setting your expectations, this allows your child to meander through the difficult moment and understand that love and peace exist. Being firm while teaching your child rules does not have to include anger, negative feelings, or chaos. By modeling your calm and peaceful manner, children do notice and model what they see.

Teach your children well is a common lyric from a popular song by Crosby, Stills & Nash. As we teach them, it is important to know how they learn. We learn in three different ways, as a kinesthetic learner (one who learns best by doing), an auditory learner (one who learns best by listening), a visual learner (one who learns best by watching), or a combination of two. Remember, being someone who learns visually may not be the same way your child learns. Figuring out how you and your child learn is essential in moving forward with your teaching of family rules.

When a situation arises where your child decides to go against the family rules, the best bet is to be sure to remind the child of the family rule, as well as the consequence that warrants the negligence. Because many youngsters like to flex their muscles in an environment other than their home, upon arrival at their own home, be sure to follow through with a discussion and consequence. This way, as you complete this battle, the child will see that their actions are monitored and consequences are always consistent. When there is a lack of follow through, the results in children's learning will demonstrate to them that they can get away with bad behavior.

Rewards and Consequences

I believe that all children come to us with their own knowledge, gifts, and attitudes. In this belief, children will thrive and grow with a sense of love if it surrounds them. I made sure that every positive or negative moment was a teachable moment. If one child began fighting with the other, I intervened in order to guide them to a reasonable outcome. Communicate the importance of working out the grievance and reminding them that being upset is allowed. Modeling how to deal with the upset is crucial.

It is important that children understand that their emotions will spark out. This reminder to them that all people feel upset every now and then is a great lesson to teach. Showing and discussing how to deal with the negative emotions in a calm way is the ultimate goal. This will give way to good sportsmanship.

One of the most important values I continually expressed out loud was the need for a peaceful climate within my four walls. I made sure my children knew that within my castle, I would only allow love, truth, and peace. Nothing else was tolerated. This was one time where I learned the true meaning of consistency. Like the Oprah saying goes, "Please be responsible for the energy you bring into this space." This restated quote by Dr. Jill Bolte Taylor hangs in my home. We remain consistent with these words.

If someone felt sad, cranky, or just out of sorts, I made sure that they knew it was ok to feel this way, but it wasn't ok to disrupt others around them. They knew they could have time alone in their room, but they couldn't use this feeling to get what they wanted. This is important because it will help them in the real world. As an athlete, it is important to show leadership, patience, and fairness. Becoming an unruly teammate can lead to harsh references when time to be selected for college, so it is crucial to teach this area on emotions early in order to be successful later.

Being Responsible for Their Moods

They were taught that they couldn't be in a bad mood in order to take over the room they shared. Selfishness was nipped in the bud immediately. Being out of sorts was one thing, however using this in order to hog the room was not going to be allowed. Simultaneously, practicing skills in life to change their mood from bad to good was taught at every chance.

Children are like sponges. They pick up and learn everything around them. In addition, they are pieces of clay that can be molded into the most outstanding individuals. Consistency comes into play here. Mold the pieces of clay with the end result in mind. All this work is important in order to help display them as adults later in life. Helping to mold independent humans is the outcome we seek.

Teaching your guidelines of your household values and rules, you must continually hold your children to those rules. Once you draw the line in the sand, it is a must to use consistent reminders with your children. Easier said than done.

If someone lashes out at another due to their cranky mood, consequences are given. If selfishness becomes the outcome when it comes to taking over a shared space, it is important to show the ramifications from their actions.

Being clear on what the consequences are in your home is step one. Never letting the offender off the hook is rule number two. Once consequences are clear, such as losing a toy, television or video time, or bike privileges, it is our job as adults to stick to them like glue. Rewards of praise and 'at-a-boys' are words that should be used every day.

Every child is sweet and has the most adorable smile, but if you do not consistently show them their consequences along with verbal praises when they cross your line, there will be no peace, joy or harmony. You can kiss goodbye the tranquil atmosphere you were trying to create.

Logical Consequences

As you create the peaceful environment you seek and have consequences established, you can see it is crucial to use logical consequences as you speak to your child. I have always taught my girls, "You can say things two different ways in the world; you can either speak with kindness or with meanness. Which way do you want to receive these thoughts?"

To help, it is important to understand what logical consequences means. Based on Center on the Social and Emotional Foundations for Early Learning/U.S Dept of Health and Human Services, logical consequences refers to the actions or responses that are implemented following a child's inappropriate behavior that serve to discourage the child from engaging in the behavior again. It is a way of speaking to the child by letting them know what they did wrong and how they should behave while showing no reprimands or scolding.

If I think back to how some teachers back in the day took care of misbehaved children, there was a lot of scolding and berating of individuals. It was sad that it occurred when I attended school, but as Oprah always says, "When you know better, you do better."

As educators and parents of the 21st century, we are aware of the damage that occurs when you demean people with words. Words are power. Words can build up or break down someone. In the Bible, Proverbs 16:24 NLT says, "Kind words are like honey-sweet to the soul and healthy for the body." Building up a child's sense of self worth is the only way we should be educating behavior from bad to good. Praise them for what they do right; let them know what behavior was incorrect, and follow through with two choices; one by doing the correct and appropriate behavior or to have an immediate consequence linked to the behavior.

For example, if little Peter is not helping to clean up the toys in order to go out and play, then he will not be able to go out and play until he shows he can clean up. Keeping him from going out to play is the consequence connected to the behavior. A threat of taking away his use of videos at another time is unfitting. So if Tara is a child who was asked to take a bath before viewing her favorite show and does not listen, missing the show is the consequence connected to the misbehavior.

In addition, it is necessary to have the child correctly have a bath and model the correct way of using the bath toys. Consistency must prevail. There must be follow through of the consequences linked to the behavior or the child will only learn that threats can be easily overcome.

Be consistent with your teaching. Be persistent in your leading. Remember to keep in your heart that God gave you these children as a gift. The gift is that they are actually here to teach you; whereas we think it's our hands that do it all. Embrace the knowledge that you will be learning lessons for yourself during this journey with your angels.

Be Firm & Consistent with Rules

As I speak to other educators, business owners of after school activities, and other parents', findings are that today's children need to be lassoed and taught along with their parents that when you make a mistake own up to it. Too many parents are quick to believe their children over a teacher or other adult in authority position.

Believe me, we all think our child was the most truthful darling around, but be honest; of course a child is going to try to convince their parent that the teacher was wrong. They know that a consequence will be given at school, so no wonder they are trying their hardest to get out of it. We have all been there. But as we all mature, hopefully we've seen the avoidance and acknowledge that our adorable little angels could be fibbing and see them trying to get their parents to take their side.

An all out war when a child commits a wrong is not the step to take. However, by matching the consequence with the action and providing the atmosphere of tranquility, they will learn that their actions have outcomes.

Live in the Truth

Some actions receive rewards and some actions receive consequences. Once they are in the environment of practicing this way of life, they begin to live with the good behavior you set out to model. You'll be able to see if this behavior is occurring when you ask at their parent/teacher conference. Usually what's taught at home shows up in the classroom.

By standing by your child when they are making wrong choices and not acknowledging their mistake, you will only add to their destruction. Without a doubt, we want our child to know that we are on their side and we always have their back, however, continuing to backup bad behavior is only teaching your child that they can make bad choices and they will not be penalized.

Not only will teachers and other adults begin to eliminate the child with bad behavior from different activities, they will also begin to miss out on fun activities with their peers. You can bet that if their behavior can harm someone else, they will find themselves alone and shunned.

Think about it, not many people want to be around others who act out negatively. The terms spoiled, bratty, and entitled are the adjectives most used around the school parking lot during pick up and drop off. This would be the time to practice dropping the ego, acknowledge your behavior as a parent taking the side of a child who is misbehaving, take responsibility for your actions and the actions of your child, and model the proper behavior for your child to learn and one day emulate.

You're Not Their Friend

Too many parents want to be their child's friend. As parents, we are their mentor, guide, safe haven, and friendly adult figure, not their friend. Our children have enough friends at school, on the soccer field, and in their neighborhood. What is most needed is someone who is willing to take the time to model good behavior and teach by showing the standard acceptable in society. That is the number one goal.

Can your child deal with the many situations in society on their own? Are they capable of figuring out what they did wrong and correct the problem? You certainly do not need a young person in their 20's hanging around your house afraid to get out into the real world. In addition, you don't want your children too comfortable having their parent take care of every little complication. In this state, they will never mature to the level of independence they need to reach in order to become a responsible adult.

By being their friend, that is exactly what you are creating for their future and yours. There is absolutely nothing wrong with being friendly, but once you cross over into the friend category, all bets are off.

Be aware and always keep in mind that children are not bad, but their behavior may be. By preserving the fact that children act a certain way at each age, a parent will save themselves some energy. During the time of the terrible twos, some parents have to deal with this burst of energy and attitude. Be ready to stand your ground, stay in peace, and remember that you are the guide and not the warden.

Let me be your crystal ball and let you in on the outcome of friend vs. friendly. By representing yourself as the friendly parent, you will see your child prosper and grow. As a parent of a child who had to endure consequences and have their internet time cancelled from time to time in order to teach a lesson, your angel will flourish into the adult with a good head on their shoulders.

If you think about it, creating flourishing adults is our main goal as parents. Seeing your adult child venture off seeking all the knowledge they can find and taking on all their responsibilities with no help from you is the outcome we all want. Be sure to state the same mantra that my family has lived by, "Yes, mother, you are not our friend, but you can be friendly!"

By acknowledging to your child that you see their untrue ways and showing them it isn't acceptable to hide their misjudgment after a wrong doing, you are preparing her to become the coachable individual that universities seek in their scholar athlete. Honesty is the best policy and no matter what, once you take their side when you know they are wrong, they will think it is acceptable. When children are taught early that a wrong decision must be acknowledged and changed, they are stepping into greatness. This is what scholar athletes are made of.

Chapter 10

Coachable Through Positive Thoughts

"The most successful people see adversity not as a stumbling block, but as a stepping-stone to greatness."

~Shawn Achor

"Being coachable means you're leaving room for the possibility that there's something you haven't learned yet that could make you even better." Laura Di Franco, a holistic physical therapist and writer, also stated that the road to being coachable involves recognizing it includes having a happy and productive life. In order to create a happy life, one has to befriend positivity.

One of my favorite quotes comes from Shawn Achor. The great ones look fear in the eyes and conquer without hesitation. They come with a drive and wisdom more excelled than the rest of us. I feel like their souls are very connected to their purpose.

Coachable athletes come from parents who helped them control their temper, understand their attitude, and learn that it involves work ethic with passion. As parents, it is our job to guide our scholar athlete towards the qualities of being coachable and showing them how to succeed in their purpose.

What Coachable Means

Research shows there are four ways to be coachable. Non coachable is a person who only takes action on their own and will not take the advice of a coach. A selectively coachable person will only take action when they agree with their coach. The reluctantly coachable person will take action from their coach in spite of their doubts and distrust, whereas a completely coachable person will take action and completely trust in the coaching process. It takes positive thoughts to become coachable.

The environment in which your child dwells creates their thoughts which will in turn create an athlete who is coachable or not coachable. When your child practices aligning their thoughts to positive thinking, they become the coachable scholar athlete university coaches are looking to join their team.

Create a Positive End Result

Positivity is probably the main quality of being coachable, yet requires many aspects. When famous coaches and players are asked what coachable means to them, they all state that it never involves negativity, the inabilities to self reflect, or not being open minded to others' ideas. One important aspect that comes to their minds is having the willingness to learn. They all know that open-mindedness is at the top of that list. Being able to take criticism and knowing that it will only make one grow is something they all had to learn. Put out in the universe the very qualities that you want your children to learn and develop as a part of their makeup. This is the making of a coachable child.

Two wonderful quotes from Wayne Dyer come to mind on this subject of attracting what you want. On the subject, Dyer stated, "You do not attract what you want, you attract what you are." If you continue to act in a negative way, negativity is what will continue to show up in your life. Because that is the energy that is being radiated, that is the energy that is radiated back to you.

In addition to that quote, Dyer also explains this idea when he said, "Keep reminding yourself: I get what I think about whether I want it or not." Here, he is expressing the idea from the wisdom of Tao Te Ching, which means the book for applying the virtue of living 'the way'.

The essence of this translation is if you change your thoughts you change your life. As we consistently put out in the universe that we don't have something but want it, we will continue not having that in our life. We actually block our manifestation. If we use positive questions such as *what if* along with good thoughts, that is what we will manifest. By doing this, you can shift your life by the way you think.

It doesn't matter how old a person is to begin this shift. It does matter that the person's intentions are expressed and released in the way in which is the most positive. Dyer teaches us that, "You create your thoughts, your thoughts create your intentions, and your intentions create your reality."

Weed Out Untrue Thoughts

If your child has bad behavior, they have the ability with their spirituality and thoughts to change their behavior from bad to good. It is the parent's job to help the child see the reality they're creating and change it through their intentions. Our intentions must be positive and backed with honesty. These aspects are the qualities of being coachable.

Bad behavior is coming from an atmosphere that is negative. We can change the atmosphere by saying to the child, "You are enough." When we put down our walls and apologize to the child for our mistakes, they feel the ability to let down theirs. Let your child know that they're enough. At this point, you will connect to them with love. Sit with them in this special connection. It is the love that shows the way. It is the love that helps us move forward toward an opened connection.

Sometimes the thoughts we think someone has about us aren't true. They are simply created in the mind to help in the story of why someone treats another a certain way. Your child may have these untrue thoughts in their head. They may think that their parents think of them in negative ways, where in fact, those thoughts were merely created by them. These false thoughts may be in their mind controlling them. They are acting out negatively over thoughts that were made up and untrue about them. In reality, these thoughts don't exist. When we help them understand these thoughts, they step closer to being coachable.

Dr. Shefali Tsabary is a well renowned clinical psychologist who has helped many families understand ways of parenting by looking at the spirit of both the parent and child by using both eastern philosophy and Western psychology. She believes that successful children experience openness, communication and love.

Children feel safe with their family. She believes that it is more important to care who they are and not so much their actions when the bad behavior appears. As you notice that your child is acting out, rest assured that this is happening because they are struggling with something.

Helping With Their Struggle

When children are consistently acting out, look at their heart and realize this behavior is usually a cry for help. They are hurting in some way and can only think to act out to get attention. We, as parents, feel torn because we know what goes along with this emotion. It is vital that we let our child's vulnerability show and embrace this. Deal with the cry for help. Let them bring it to the surface.

Sometimes the feeling of hurt is coming to the surface because a child is feeling lonely. This loneliness can come from many parts of their day. They may be below grade level and struggling with keeping up with the work load. They may feel lonely because parents work many hours and they feel neglected. They may be bullied at school and too ashamed to speak out. At this point, put a halt to all things in your life. Stop and evaluate where you are in life and pay attention to what is actually happening. We tend to cover up the real with unrealistic.

For example, if you were living in a house that's too hard to pay for, or a car too expensive, or simply a lifestyle that cannot

Let Down Your Wall

Let down your wall and see your child's true feelings. When your wall comes down, so does theirs. This creates a connection based on love and honesty. Explain to the child that sometimes thoughts that are untrue are created by their feelings. Connecting with them helps keep those untrue thoughts from forming and love becomes present. The love helps keep the positive energy flow between parent and child.

By taking the steps toward a positive end result made up of good intentions, you are helping to manifest their future. As you let your wall down, be open with your own examples. Let them hear how you once took untrue thoughts to heart and how they created negative actions that never had to occur. Explain how you understand what keeps these thoughts out of your mind. In addition, as you speak about your own life lessons, they see that others had to do the work and it isn't such a lonely and scary place.

If your child consistently stays in the bad behavior, their intentions must be changed. By supporting the bad behavior, the child's reality is boosted because you are allowing them to feed off the reaction they receive from you. As you support the bad behavior, they feel a sense of "good job" from you when they should be pointed in the right direction. Remember, the longer you, the adult and parent, continue to let your child behave poorly, the more likely the child will continue to behave poorly in adulthood.

In order to create a successful adult, it is crucial to work out the bad behavior. Whether it is through parental involvement of scheduling consistent meetings or counseling, it is imperative to indicate to the child that your goal is to see positive behavior and nothing else.

As someone who has worked in schools, it seems like there is a significant increase in this type of parenting. There is no longer a high respect for educators from many parents willing to take the side of their child over a competent and professional adult. There are many incidences occurring when a child's behavior in the classroom is so bad, but the parents are unwilling to acknowledge the problem.

Demonstrate Honesty as a Parent

Denial is usually the first step for some parents. They either know there is a big problem but refuse to take action, or they truly think their child is an angel, because that is their behavior in the presence of their parent. My advice to parents is to take some time to monitor their child at school by showing up unannounced to the child's class and get a real-life image of what is actually happening during recess time.

Teachers are never excited to approach a parent about a child because of possible backlash. When you take time to show up and see with your own eyes the behavior of your child, your child will realize that they have to change their actions.

Sadly, life's ups and downs have an effect on youngsters. As the case may be, when this is the situation, meeting it head on is always the answer. Burying your head in the sand is the worst avenue to travel. Parents may not realize how many different people in a school district can help out in these somber and distressed times.

Take a deep breath and recognize the problem. Acknowledge in your heart that it is in no way a reflection of your parenting, and ask for help. Being open and honest is the best medicine. Allow yourself to let what is already planned from our Divine happen. Practice going with the flow. Keep in mind that this

is a lesson to learn. Walk into the space with an opened heart, positive intentions, and peace so that your child will learn.

Coachable Students Emulate Their Parents

Because our children are like sponges, they are aware of what we do and emulate those actions. We watched them do this as babies and now they are doing it as pre-teenagers. Since they will imitate our actions and thinking, it is vital to be the parent who models coachable qualities. Michael Jordan says, "My best skill was that I was coachable. I was a sponge and aggressive to learn". Coming from the king of coachable, his words are valuable to parents because they state what is in the mind of a successful athlete who is coachable.

If you show disrespect or quitting, those are qualities your children may pick up. It's all about showing them their path towards success. Vince Lombardi, one of the greatest coaches in football and a national icon whose name is on the Super Bowl trophy, believed in an athlete's dedication and effort. He once stated, "Once you learn to quit, it becomes a habit". Another famous quote of his is, "The only place success comes before work is in the dictionary." As we can see, great players have the high qualities that a great coach is looking for.

Successful Children Come from Open Parents

Being coachable means having the quality of open-mindedness. Since open-mindedness means having the quality to be receptive to new ideas and opinions, these people are able to hear what they're doing wrong and seek to make themselves better without controversy.

be reached with your funds, you should step back and breathe. Be honest with your circumstances. As you claw and struggle to hold onto things that are too hard to keep in your life, notice the negativity it creates and start letting them go.

In order to solve the problems of your lonely and hurting child, it may be that you need to find a smaller and more affordable house. It may be that your car should be traded in for a used one and one more affordable. This takes the pressure off of constantly leaving your children with others to raise and you becoming the parent you always wanted to become.

It doesn't matter where you live or what you drive. Those thoughts are yours. Those are your beliefs formed by others. Form your own beliefs. Believe in your thoughts, your children, and your needs. It may be a fact that you change these things so that you can spend more time with your hurting child. This change will find you helping your hurting child climb out of their loneliness and bad behavior. Isn't that worth it? Isn't that the parent you always wanted?

By changing your thoughts, you can change your life and possibly the lives around you. By downsizing, you may have the time to be with the lonely child. You may now have the funds to find someone to help such as a tutor or a counselor. You may experience the only important thing in life is family and not the objects. You may find that collecting your angels and nurturing them is the reason why you are here, and not the collecting of things to impress others.

Practice Mindful Parenting

As humans with egos, we want to hide the vulnerability of our child because we are taught that it is a sign of weakness. Whereas, the lesson for parents is seeing the truth of vulnerability in a different light. In fact, by noticing your vulnerability and letting it out, we tend to deal with the problem that brought out the vulnerable side in us.

Dr. Shefali states that we need to take notice of the feelings that arise in us when our child has a meltdown. She has learned that we must look at the whole picture of the occurrence. If someone yells at us, Dr. Shefali says we need to think about what we would want at that moment and supply that to our own inner child.

Dr. Shefali believes that it is important for us to look at the spirit of our children and act upon them from that side. By taking a step back and living in the fact that we as parents don't know everything, we are creating the peaceful space for both the child and parent to learn without the negative thoughts that only pressure, mistakes, and criticism exist.

As we help our children, we must remember to treat their spirits with tenderness the same way we would a baby bird's injured wing. We give it love, help it develop and grow, and let it spread on its own. When we offer these to our child, they become part of the coachable aspects they will need later.

"Difference between school and life: School teaches you lessons then gives you the test. Life gives you the test and you learn the lesson." Always be connected to why you are here and why these situations are coming up in your life. Slow down and seek the lesson. Use your knowledge, ask the Divine to point you in the right direction, and constantly be mindful that a lesson is available for you to learn. Some people use the strategies of counting to ten or going to their happy place when they find themselves in a dark spot. Find what works for you and incorporate it.

A Joyful Mindset is Coachable

Our minds cannot think both a positive and negative thought at the same time. So the lesson here is the more you fill your brain with positive thoughts, the less chance there is to have a negative one. One might think this is too easy. Nowhere does it say that finding your peace has to come from a hard place.

This strategy is perfect when you are seeking to live in a joyful mindset. Instruct your mind to think of only positive thoughts. The negative ones may pop into mind when you forget to monitor your positive ones, but once more select only positive and joyous thoughts. Enjoy the good feeling you have when your poised reflection comes into mind. Practice embracing that feeling. Hold that composed sensation.

Sounds simple so some people may think it is hogwash. On the contrary, do the uncomplicated strategy and giggle at the fact that it is so easy. When you feel that way, you know you are on the right track to help them become coachable.

Chapter 11

Cut the Cord of Technology

"That the more kids watch TV before the age of three, the more likely they are to have attention problems in school."

~**Dr. Christakis**

Children, who have too much stimulus in their environment on a constant basis, will experience negative effects in their success as students.

If I'm a parent with a baby of a few months reading this, I think I would stop in my tracks. If I'm a parent of a child in elementary school, my mouth might drop to the floor. But if I'm a parent of a child in middle school, I would feel my eyes bulging out.

At this point, you may be reviewing in your head the entire collection of technology that you have available for your baby or child. These may be in the form of a tablet, television, and smart phone. Your heart might be racing at the fact that you've introduced these to your angel and your next thought is how hard it will be to cut the cord. Simply take a breath or two. Keep in mind; what's done is done. There is time to undo anything to help get your child back on course.

As you read the following research found on the significance these devices have on our children, learn from the findings and know that I will help devise a plan for your family. The plan will include the 21 day habitual method from Chapter 3 along with introducing scheduling into their day as well as consistency and the CIO method while introducing the new rules of device usage to the family. It definitely sounds scary and a lot of work, but this shows how my four keys work in so many circumstances.

Old School as the New School of Thought

Based on research, we are finding out that noise hinders how children learn. In her findings, Dr. Rochelle Newman states that children learn language from hearing it, but too much noise is something that children's brains can't process.

If we look at research on age with how long children watch and listen to television daily, Dr. Dimitri Christakis, a professor of pediatrics at the University of Washington, discovered that, "In 1970, the average age at which children watched television was four years. Today, the average age is four months."

His studies have linked television viewing to the overstimulation of an infant's brain with further findings that this may lead to ADHD (Attention-Deficit/Hyperactivity Disorder) developing in our young children. He has also determined that the brain triples in size in the first two years of life, so connections that are formed in the brain are based on their early life experiences.

He has further stated that, "Prolonged exposure to rapid image change during critical period of brain development would precondition the mind to expect high levels of stimulation and that would lead to inattention in later life." In other words, plopping your child at a very early age in front of the television or even with a smart phone is a definite way of hurting your child's future success in school. If they can't pay attention in class, their capacity and ability to retain and learn will be low.

It is vital to think about your infant's brain on a daily basis. Are you over stimulating? Are you putting the proper nutrition into your infant's body and brain? Are you giving your angel the best environment in order for them to prosper throughout all grade levels?

These questions need to be addressed each day. There is so much research out there that we can't ignore anymore. Looking at the info collected from 2011 to 2013 alone, the increase in device usage for children 8 and under is staggering.

The report on two year olds using mobile devices for media has elevated at an alarming rate. The findings *from Zero to Eight: Children's Media Use in America 2013*, Common Sense Media states, "72% percent of children 8 and under have used a mobile device for some type of media activity such as playing games, watching videos, or using apps, up from 38% percent in 2011." Their research also showed that, "38% of children under 2 years old have used a mobile device for media compared to 10% two years ago."

Technology = ADD

Information on this subject showing research to 2019 is heart stopping to educators and parents alike. Not only are we seeing increases in special needs such as ADD, ADHD, and focusing problems, but there is now a rise in student caused injuries nationwide. As parents, we must take a stand starting in our homes.

In his studies, Dr. Christakis described, "That the more kids watch TV before the age of three, the more likely they are to have attention problems in school." He has also acknowledged that, "For every hour watching television, a child under the age of three increases the chances to have attention problems later with 10%."

We are killing our children's brains and how they function with every minute we put them in front of the television or any technological device screen. It is imperative to eliminate TV and screen viewing with our very young children and replace it with real play time.

Hand eye coordination toys, touching blocks, and moving around these objects with their own movements are the activities that should be in front of them. Eliminating all screen time is necessary at this very young age.

They will have plenty of time to learn how a computer and all technologies work. Television should only be used for educational purposes and for only a very short period of time. Letting an infant explore their environment with their own senses is key at the early stage of their growing brain.

As I look back, television was not on when I was a stay at home mom. Once they were about two years old, they viewed PBS and their educational programming. We also only showed Disney singing videos that they would sing with while they would stack their blocks or color.

After hearing this, every parent should be trying every strategy to keep their children from falling into this scary environment. If the child's brain grows the most up to age two and even more until the age of five, be the parent and put your foot down.

Back in the day when I grew up, we had the beginning of video games on the television, walkman cassette players, and cable for television. Moms had to put their foot down as this new technology started. Lay down the rules of how much device use will occur in your household and don't waver. You are the parent, act like one. This is the most important topic. You are in charge of how your child's brain grows.

Device Control

Yes, it will be hard at first if your young two year olds have experienced using your device. They will cry and possibly have a meltdown. They will act out because you are creating change in their wants. Stay calm and focus on the fact that changing their environment will help them achieve more. As they fight back because they are addicted to the device, breathe, smile, and remind yourself that this is for their good.

A great place to start would be to review chapter 3 and use the information in the section of the 21 day habitual method. You will be starting a new change in a new stage of your child. As stated before, create the rules for your child of when and where their use of devices is allowed. Be ready for the change to ruffle up their feathers.

There isn't any way to go back in time and undo the attention problems of your child. However, now that you are aware of how your child's brain develops, take every little step in every way to make a huge impact.

Restructuring Technology at Home

By reviewing Chapter 3 and creating a new schedule using consistency, this is the step towards revamping and redoing what was started by allowing so much technology. It is an addiction. It must be treated as such. Using consistent strategies, parents must present with fragile gloves understanding that it will not happen overnight. It will take many weeks, but isn't it worth a few weeks of uncomfortable in order to help our children restructure their brains for success?

A parent's mind will be asking, "How long will this take? Will it ruin any kind of relationship we have now? What is the end outcome after creating such significant change in their life?" Please understand that it will take time, but there will be a happy result. It turns out fine.

As you begin usage scheduling, have other forms of fun available such as classical music playing while your children complete homework at the table or in the living room. Have board games, magazines, and books available in reach for them to explore. Have available mind thinking games, such as SKIP BO, Ticket to Ride, Risk, and Telestrations, where they use drawing or strategizing to replace their device giving them a break for awhile.

Be sure they have a magazine, comic book or actual book at their nightstand instead of the phone or Kindle. Help them start a new habit of charging their phone away from the bed so it isn't easily accessed. Research shows that if someone awakes in the middle of the night and look at their device, it adds to longer insomnia. Hopefully, this habit will extend when they are away at college.

Strategies without Technology

Arrange a time when homework is completed and schedule time with them to check it. Let them know that as the homework and any project is completed, they may use a device for a set amount of time. By authorizing this special usage time, they will connect it to a positive outcome of completing school work.

When a parent creates these checks and balances similar to what they have at school, they become more responsible for their work. This also helps set up a schedule in the household for children to follow. They will put more thought into their projects and be willing to ask more questions. Not only are you setting boundaries, but they will feel more comfortable to reach out to you.

In order for the restructuring to work, it is up to the parents. Homework time must be a priority. When other outside functions come up, homework time needs to be evaluated. If it is an important paper or studying for an upcoming test, it should be scheduled and students must understand that fun activities might be missed. It is part of the fun of being a parent. By making this time a priority as it correlates with their technology time, it will have a great impact on the family as a whole.

As they grew older, we had to monitor our children's television time. This is where consistency came into play at this stage. Sticking to your rules is crucial. Peeking into their rooms, asking questions, and offering outdoor options in activities actually works when your children are high school age. Yes, we use our manners by knocking and showing our respect, and the push back can become harsh, but stick to your plan and breathe.

While we were restructuring our rules with technology as technology grew, we started delving into their likes and interests. While they were fully engaged in their sports, there were breaks to plan times offering old school strategies. One daughter loved world history and was following her path of becoming an archaeologist. We found awesome shows on the History Channel and made time to sit and watch with her as we learned.

As she attended college back east, we heard about King Tut exhibits and other museum happenings, bought tickets, and attended with her. The best advice I can give here is to let them tell you all they are learning. It is an eye opener. It was so fulfilling and incredible to hear everything she learned. As she was our guide around the exhibit and telling us different facts, others heard her and started following. She started her own tour with many visitors walking with her asking questions. This is the pay off. This is the tremendous outcome you receive as you use consistency with your children when it comes to cutting the cord of technology. Their true selves burst out.

Chapter 12

The Power of Technology

"Technology is a useful servant but a dangerous master."

~Christian Lous Lange

"We're changing the world with technology", said Bill Gates. William S. Burroughs said, "The purpose of technology is not to confuse the brain but to serve the body." At the medical level, technology can help treat and save more people with today's harmful bacteria as well as increase productivity of industry in the world. As parents, it is up to us to help teach our children the good and bad qualities of today's technology.

Take the Good with the Bad

As a former reading teacher, and a special education teacher working with students who are below grade level, I can see how technology is giving our learners benefits, yet helping to keep them at the level they are with no hope of increasing. Yes, some students will increase their knowledge and achieve grade level, however children with attention disabilities will have a hard time moving on in the technology based world we live in.

On the one hand, being able to show a visual on a particular bat cave that we're reading about in class is so amazing and helpful for my students. However, I do understand the research out there that shows how the Internet is harmful due to the fact that it inhibits our children of thinking: such as attention, imagination, and memory/learning. As parents, these qualities are the ones we want our children to possess. So, if the Internet and technology are going to decrease their thinking, which is the gateway to all the qualities one needs to be successful in school, what is a parent to do?

Dr. Jim Taylor, PhD, who teaches at the University of San Francisco, specializes in the psychology of business, sport, and parenting. He stated, "The ability of your children to learn to focus effectively and consistently lays the foundation for almost all aspects of their growth and is fundamental to their development into successful and happy people." He goes on to state that the immediate environment of children determines the kind of attention they develop.

As I taught reading, I found that students, who hated reading because they weren't reading topics that they enjoyed, began loving it once they discovered their favorite topics in books. They became avid readers. These students realized how much of their imagination was used. In fact, reading helps in the areas of reflection, critical thinking, problem solving and vocabulary. Keep in mind these are the same qualities of being coachable. It is also found that presentations with text- only are more engaging, entertaining, and more informative than one with only video. It has also been researched that lessons and info given to the students with video and internet access were not being recalled and they weren't performing well on the test.

Balance and Responsibility

However, let's not pull the cord altogether. On the other hand, it is found that our children are learning differently. Students are more likely to learn and recall where and how to find the answer rather than remembering a high level of information. The Internet is also teaching our youngsters how to skim and see only the important information that they need. Research shows that by doing this, these young learners can engage in critical thinking and problem solving better since they don't need to retain so much information.

Since so many school districts are stating that they are embracing the future of technology and also the concept of critical thinking and problem solving, research shows that technology can increase these important attributes, but it must be done at a balance. Students must continue to learn how to hear lectures, take notes, and learn from lectures vs. power points that have too many videos and links. Schools should use different technology based lessons on such sites as Nearpod, Storybird, and Brainpop. However, these classroom tools should be used in addition to lectures and notes.

With the focus of using technology, districts should also have classes that teach responsible use of these devices and how harmful they can be to youngsters. By planting this knowledge into their brains now, whether college or trade school bound, students need to be taught the effects and harmful outcomes of using these devices exclusively. We, as parents, can have a big impact on what students do on the Internet. By teaching students at a young age how technology can be harmful to their brain, these students will become more responsible for themselves.

Don't get me wrong, there were times when I was ill, but still had to watch my girls. Yes, these were the times where I put in movies to watch, since I wasn't able to take them to the park. There will be times when they become ill with painful earaches. Again, you will find yourselves as parents going against your rules in order to help them take their mind off their illness.

Monkey See Monkey Do

Your child will follow your example, not your advice. I am glad my children shadowed what they saw. This is an important lesson for parents. Knowing our children watch us and learn from our actions is rewarding for parents.

If we are preaching no texting while driving, we must make sure we are the models as parents. You can bet they will not text and drive. I have always showed my girls that cell phones don't belong in our hands while we drive. I have always modeled putting them in the console or back seat. My phone only gets answered by someone else when I'm driving. When I see Snapchats or pictures of them driving at college, I'm always the one asking if they text and drive. I love hearing their wonderful sarcastic answers, "No mom, I don't want to die at my own hands. I have worked too hard this semester."

The Addiction of Technology

Our new technology today is addicting. As moms, we need to be consistent on our rules when it comes to Smartphone usage with our young ones. Yes, as a mom, you may need a break and use the internet to calm the young ones. Find educational programs similar to a "Mr. Rogers'. Dr Christakis has a wonderful Tedx Talk laying out how a child's brain grows, how technology can hurt it, and the outcome of what happens to a brain under such a high level of stimulus.

He teaches us how the vibration and motions on the screens are addicting to our youngsters. A steady feeding of this makes us feel like we need to have this constantly. As Dr. Christakis states in his video, "We as adults try to make narratives out of the crazy children videos, but with all that screen change, all that stimulation keeps them (children) engaged in the screen." Because babies are watching Baby Einstein or similar videos, they don't have the capability to form any kind of narrative. Just because they look attentive, doesn't mean they're learning anything. Their actions may look focused, but in actuality, they aren't learning anything except how to deal with such a large amount of screen changes on its brain. Like Dr. Christakis explains, "We are only conditioning the mind to that reality which doesn't actually exist."

It is the rapid sequencing that our children are becoming addicted to having. Even though his Tedx Talk video was released in 2011, his findings still stand. Christakis researched how programs with no rapid screen changes, like Mr. Rogers, and ones with parental guidance markings for rapid changes, such as PowerPuff Girls, stand up to each other on the basis of increasing risks and attention problems in school age children. The findings were amazing but of course made sense. Mr. Rogers videos posed no threat whereas the rapid videos such as Powerpuff Girls and violent game videos posed a 60% to 110% increase in risk of attention problems for our children.

With all this information, why aren't we taking a stand on this with our children? Have we forgotten who the parent is and who is the child? We wouldn't let them continuously eat a cup of sugar every day for breakfast. Certainly, we would put a stop to that immediately.

As wonderful researchers are all coming up with the same advice, such as Dr. Christakis, Jim Taylor, PhD, Boston University School of Medicine, and The American Academy of Pediatrics, it is now our job as parents to walk our child into their current path. If they were walking straight into oncoming traffic, we'd throw ourselves out there to save them. If they were ready to eat a poisonous detergent pod, we'd dive towards them covering their mouths.

With all this research, info, and Tedx Talk videos on the subject of technology being harmful to our children's brains, why aren't we diving at the smartphones and devices to hit them out of their hands and vision?

The Cognitive Answer

After watching and reading up on all the information available, the answer is more cognitive stimulation. Fun and simple ideas such as reading, singing, block building, rings, live puppet show, and trips to museums are the best cognitive answer as your scholar athlete grows and matures . Having children's books made out of cloth or plastic laminated pages are great for the tub and looking at in the living room with the television off. Parents who read from their own books or magazines show children how to read with others.

Of course, singing while bathing and playing are great ways to create peace. Great examples of hand to eye coordination is using building blocks or rings with soothing classical or meditation music in the background. Attending a live puppet show is a perfect example of reality in real motion and visiting a museum is the best way to see how to learn besides in a classroom or on a computer.

While I met friends for breakfast one morning, my friend's little two year old was enjoying her pancakes. However, through her meal, she pulled at her mom's phone and talked her mom into watching something. I did notice that after a while, she actually became bored with it. I reached out to the small butter bowl and turned it upside down. Next, I started putting them back into the small saucer one by one. She took notice and began doing the same thing. She started doing this for the next 20 minutes. This is what children at the age of two needs. They should be practicing to use their small finger muscles along with hand-eye coordination.

Seeing real artifacts is what set my daughter onto her path of archaeology. Seeing shark documentaries and visiting shark teeth at surf shops sent my other daughter on her path. Attending cooking classes at our local Michael's store started my youngest on her path of cake decorating. She flips through cooking magazines and the archaeologist does the same thing in her craft. Show them that there are more than just computers and smartphones. There's a whole world for them waiting to teach them and show them anything they want to learn.

Cognitive Skills Increase Brain's Abilities

As the award of our babies experiencing this kind of stimulation, there is a drop in attention problems later in school years. Each hour dropped the risk of inattention by 30% on a daily basis. It really is up to us as parents to help teach them what goes in their mouths and brains as nutrition.

Not only does technology affect our child's brain, but as young parents, we use it around our infant too much. Even when we are walking our child in their stroller or harness, what we have our mind and intention on is the key to our peace. We must be aware of the environment of their ears and ours.

As we were relaxing on the beach, my husband and I saw a young couple walking on the beach with their infant. As the precious arms and legs dangled out of the snuggly that was worn on the man, both adults had their phones in hand held out putting all their attention on it and not each other. I wanted to say, "You'll have plenty time later to look at your phone! Hold each others' hand, whisper or hum to your little one, and just enjoy where you are! Take in some big breaths, connect, and don't worry about the outside world. It's always right there."

Understandably, this could've been their first time on their phones because of the crying and screaming that might've taken place on the way to the beach. But come on, make connections with each other. Believe me, the less time you make for your significant other will turn out to be the answer to why there is no relationship when they grow up and leave for college. Create loving moments even if they will only be for a few minutes. It will pay off in the long run.

In the end, we can help our children live happy and healthy. When you begin this difficult change with consistency and love, there will always be a happy ending. Remember, we are all human beings who just want to know that we are being heard, felt, and that we matter to the one we love. Most need to connect with touch, conversation, and words. When you find your children at a point in the day when they are doing fine, seek out your mate and give them your time. Time is precious here on Earth, don't waste it.

Chapter 13

Emotional Intelligence IQ vs. EQ

"Gifted leadership occurs when heart and head— feeling and thought meet. These are the two winds that allow a leader to soar."

~David Goleman

Back in the 1990's, Daniel Goleman was a psychologist and science reporter who stumbled onto an article by two other psychologists about the concept of "emotional intelligence". At this time, the standard of excellence in life was a person's IQ. But suddenly, there was a new idea that made more sense when it came to a person's success in life. It wasn't just the amount and quality of knowledge that a person possessed, but the overall quality of book smarts with the social and emotional intelligence a person acquired.

This idea became more apparent when Goleman wrote his book laying out the significance of emotional intelligence and how it would help, not only in the workforce, but in the everyday life of a child's classroom.

Back in the day, 'smart' used to mean that the smarter you were, the more likely you would attend Harvard or Princeton. Your IQ was thought to be in the genes of highly positioned individuals and possibly fostered by experience. But with this new way of thinking came the possibility that our emotions were connected and needed to be present in our intelligence.

EQ is the New IQ

With the help of David Goleman's book, *Emotional Intelligence, Why it can matter more than IQ*, it became apparent that success in life and work is (based) on much more than IQ. In 1995, not only did EI or emotional intelligence and SEL programs become adopted into schools and into curriculum, but this concept spread worldwide. A decade later, SEL programs (Social and Emotional Learning) went from a small introduction in schools to thousands of schools adopting this new way of thinking worldwide.

Some believe as a child learns these EQ or EI, Emotional Intelligence, it can enhance the school environment from one of violence, bullying, drugs, and poor discipline to one that promotes and increases a student's academic performance. Research found that by helping children improve their self-awareness and confidence along with learning to manage their emotions, impulses, and empathy, they also show improved academic scores and achievement.

This improvement was found when schools tracked their achievement scores. They found that there was a 50 percent increase in children's scores and a 38 percent increase in their overall grade point average. This improvement is exciting to see! These numbers tell the story that it isn't only smarts that make up the intelligence of a person, but the emotional feelings and emotional environment in which these children learn. EQ improves the overall being.

Seeing that schools are taking these pieces of research and incorporating them into the day of a student is reassuring to me as a parent and educator. Even more so, seeing the highly accredited business publication such as *The Harvard Business Review* embrace this knowledge of emotional intelligence gives hope for it to inspire all businesses to follow suit.

Teaching Self-Awareness

Today, the emotional intelligence movement is in the lives of our children as SEL in schools' curriculum. SEL stands for social and emotional learning. It is a way for students to recognize and manage their emotions in themselves and others. It teaches empathy for others as well as teaching them to control their impulses. SEL helps students learn to communicate with others clearly and assertively, yet keeping the other individual's feelings in mind. Students also learn to make responsible decisions and become more effective problem solvers.

Now is your turn as a parent to help your child in the SEL world of theirs. Many of these SEL skills are found during the school day when students are put into groups in order to practice working together to find answers and solve problems.

It may be used in math class when students are paired within a smaller group. They tackle a word problem and compare their answers by identifying and presenting their problem solving strategies used. Students may also use their social emotional learning while they put together a power point with their group, when researching a science application, or an important individual from our history.

Communication is the key for all students during these projects and group work in school. They have the opportunity to flex their leadership skills and their empathy towards the ideas of others. When they fail to use communication in these groups at school, others can view who can work under these particular circumstances. A student and teacher can see who can work under pressure, which student needs help to interact with others, and who is shy but becomes part of the ongoing conversation of the group.

A light bulb moment for parents can come out of this observation. In the workforce, adults have to be able to communicate in a friendly and caring manner with other coworkers. When someone doesn't see how others are feeling because of the lack of empathy they have, they are unable to hold employment. As people in the workforce, we understand how important it is to have these qualities to be successful at making a living. By working on our child's ability to communicate and understand the feelings of others is by far one of the most important areas where our children need to master while in school.

As a parent, find time to ask your child what they are working on in school. Begin to start an equal sharing of your own feelings in order to gain their trust. Letting them know some of your weaknesses you had in school can help children feel safe enough to share theirs. Information can come from the teacher or message on their web page. Some schools use an agenda where students write down their homework assignments daily.

Questioning your child on their feelings of their progress in these groups is important to investigate how well their EI/EQ is working. During your teacher conferences for your student is a great opportunity to find out how your student's social and emotional well being is being exercised. The areas your child needs help within their EQ can be practiced at home.

Bringing up problems to solve on the weekend may help give your child that one on one help needed to allow them to work well with others in their project groups at school. An example might be playing a new board game or doing a puzzle with many pieces. Both of these ideas may not be of interest to either of you, yet is perfect for this lesson. Children are put into groups and given projects to work on that are unusual. This is the perfect time to model how to work with others.

Show your child how to talk to others when feeling frustrated and ask questions for understanding. By you speaking out loud and having them repeat your words would be brilliant. It gives your child real life practice. If your child begins to become upset or frustrated to the point that they show tears or anger, validate their feelings and show them how they can be successful even when they are feeling frustrated and upset.

Modeling to your child how to be assertive yet have empathy toward another can be accomplished in the home environment. The key is to support your child by maneuvering through these learning years in areas they need improvement. I wish more parents knew that the more their child experiences at home truly helps them at school. This is why being a guiding parent is so important.

Get to Know Your Child's Passion

EQ/EI helps students understand and work through their behavior issues. By learning social and emotional skills, teachers and parents are guiding our children to become ready for their life mission. We need to educate not only their minds, but their hearts. When you discover their passions in life, use these topics to practice this idea.

Globally, EI has been taken on by top companies worldwide to enrich their employees' social and emotional skills. It must encourage parents knowing that the EI movement is not just a fad and is used routinely worldwide when hiring, promoting, and developing their employees because that will be their children one day.

Knowing that this concept exists in the workforce, it creates a sense of peace for me as an educator. Not only does it alert the world that a brain full of knowledge is not the end all be all. It shows us that the world is beginning to open hearts and minds and acknowledge a person's whole package. It is a wonderful feeling to see the world embrace the heart and soul of beings and not only the amount of knowledge stored and regurgitated.

Because this is an everyday aspect in the business world, it inspires me to know that even students, who are not at grade level but who work especially hard, can use their emotional intelligence to be as successful as a student at grade level. These social-emotional skills assist our children in becoming successful in school, the workplace, and their life.

As you can see, by monitoring your child's social-emotional learning, you are preparing them for the real world. In the real world, problem solving and communication are areas that need to exist for a company to be profitable. Learning what interests and excites your child, use these to have them practice understanding feelings of others. Even going to a museum or trade show of their interest has them practicing speaking to others as well as venturing through large groups in public.

In addition, SEL helps people resolve problems in their personal life as well as increase their performance in communication with coworkers just like family members. As your child learns these important skills within their school's curriculum, they will be ready to face the world and be successful.

By showing value for our emotional areas in life, the more valued we feel. As we teach the importance of emotional intelligence, the more valued our children will feel. By feeling cherished by those around them, our angels truly feel they can conquer all adversity. Instead of wanting to run from adversity, our children learn to stand toe to toe with their problems and meet them head on.

In today's world of technology, stressful moments can arise with the thought of firing off an angry email. As children learn the proper social-emotional skills, they grow up avoiding this impulse to lash out and decide to use their calming skills. Parents need to see that they are a big part of this solution and training. When parents are on their devices during walks, in the car, and during shopping experiences, their child is missing out on all the real life moments where they can learn empathy.

Ways to Help Your Child Progress in School

All children have the same wants and needs. Not all students look forward to doing homework, especially if it is in an area where they struggle. It is important to help your student connect with the reason why they should do the work and how that can connect to the outcome of learning.

For example, an elementary student may be struggling in writing. If we think back to our own time in school, some of us can relate. They are given a prompt to write and now enter the problem. They might not know how to go about putting words on paper. Showing them different organizers helps them actually put their words on paper.

An organizer is a way to use different boxes on paper labeled with the different parts of a writing piece. (See nancyfetzer.com and view her literacy and learning methods.) These organizers are boxes drawn on paper where every box represents a certain part of the writing such as hook, main idea, details, and topic sentences with supporting sentences along with an area for the conclusion. As students master the different areas, they practice putting these sections together in a sequential order on their chromebook or on paper to create paragraphs.

When a student can connect why they are practicing to write different types of essays (narrative, opinion, and expository), look them up on line or ask the teacher what they entail, and then little by little connect why they write. Bottom line, ask your child's teacher for a sample organizer they may use with the class and one filled out.

An example when they might need to tell a story about themselves will be on a college application. When practicing to write a narrative in elementary school, it will help them accomplish this down the road in their education as they move through high school. If they are not looking at attending college, remind them that any trade school or job application asks for the same type of writing. By showing them that what they learn will connect to their future, it may help to motivate your student.

Remind them that being able to tell the story about themselves will help them later get into a trade school or be selected for employment. Pick up a job application from a local business in your area or go on line to find one. Show your child some of the questions.

Let them feel what it's like in the real world and what they are working towards. Help them realize that everything they try to accomplish later in life is determined by their success in elementary writing class. Sometimes, a child just needs to hear why they are learning something in order to connect it to their own lives.

Keep Calm and Do Your Homework

Homework is the worst! Most children probably have a dog so they can have them eat their homework. Parents probably like the word in-law better than homework. They find the same routine everyday when it comes to the dreaded homework. Children start to act out, parents start to stress, and the wonderful evening dreamed about disappears in an instant.

Think back to a time when you avoided the dreaded H word. It is important to realize what turned you around. Falling grades, being grounded, or missing an important school function are all events that happened to us at one time or another. Being upfront and honest is the best start.

Gathering your children together and sitting them down to a family meeting is an idea that will create change. It is important for parents to hold their children accountable for their grades as well as their behavior and make sure that they are aware of the consequences that will occur when school work is incomplete and rules are broken.

Even though these strategies for homework focus on students with ADHD, Autism, or Aspergers, a subtype of autism, any of the following ideas can work with any student. Although aspergers is a subtype of autism, ADHD is not.

I have found that children with aspergers will not lie when asked a direct question. Most children just want to please their teachers and parents. While I am tutoring or teaching in the Learning Center at school, I might ask a student a specific question about how they completed an assignment. Students will generally tell the truth. The key is to ask in a friendly manner without any judgment or criticism. Students, who find themselves backed in a corner, need to feel safe and see a way out of any wrong doing. Trust is a needed tool in order to get to the reasons why someone does something.

Heart Felt Questioning that Works

I usually state, "I need to ask you a question. Please answer truthfully." Remember to wear a broad smile. When they admit to doing a test question in a lazy manner by only answering part of the question, or they're honest about not completing their homework, it is important to help them feel secure by listening.

Listening to why they did mediocre work is critical to gaining their trust. Once your child realizes that they can tell the truth and not feel defeated, use this comfortable atmosphere to explain why their unsatisfactory assignments are unacceptable.

Be aware that there will be tears and frustration. Keeping a calm attitude helps your child stay unruffled. Remind your child in a tranquil voice that crying is reserved for falling, when one hurts one's self, or when there is a death. Express to the child that feeling sad and frustrated is normal and they have a right to those emotions.

During this interaction, your child learns not only how to deal with their own self emotions, but they learn how to have empathy for others. At this moment, you are the lesson your child needs to see.

Use Their Strengths to Uplift

Start to empower them with their strengths. Break down all the good things they accomplished on their assignment. Even though a short answer was written with only one example when the question asked for several, mention all successful parts written. If the writing has good transitions and the one example is backed up with clear evidence from the passages and research, identify these significant achievements.

Now is a perfect time to speak to your child in a motivating manner. If you are unsure what to say, take some time to go online and research inspirational quotes. View them as images and locate the ones that would help your child feel energized as well as match the values that represent your family. Printing some out and hanging them on the bathroom mirror or in their bedroom is a great reminder of the power and love around them.

Unfortunately, not all children will respond the way we want on the first try. They may lash out, throw a tantrum, and make life a negative place for parents. Reach inside and remember that they are just upset and frustrated because they either don't understand something, or they are feeling fear and can't think of a way to get out of their distress.

Isaiah 44:3-4 says, "I will pour My Spirit on your descendants, and My blessing on your offspring. They will spring up among the grass like willows by the watercourses." When you feel that your road with your child in this area is not going to be pretty, reach out for God.

A wonderful book for parents in this situation is *Pray Big for Your Child, The Power of Praying God's Promises for Your Child's Life*. It is an amazing book that shows parents how to help their children by using scripture. Likewise, it teaches parents by including a daily guide and reminders for them to pray for their children every day. This book will not only help you feel peace in this trying time, but you will be demonstrating to your child how to get back to a great place.

Remind children that they can lose their job in the real world if they don't complete their work. Children must begin to hear these ideas at home. Parents waiting for schools to discipline their children are about to have a rude awakening.

Yes, it is true that in today's world, it is crucial for both parents to work. Let them know that if homework isn't complete, they don't get to attend important occasions or school events important to them. It is your job as a parent to enforce the rules in a calm manner. Show your children that you mean business.

Remember, once you carry out a consequence and your child sees the outcome of their laziness or their disregard to their school work, they begin to learn the lesson. (If needed, return to Chapter 9, *Rewards and Consequences: Be Friendly, Not Their Friend, section Rewards & Consequences*)

Children Are Not Their Grade

Another realization that parents need to address to their children when it comes to writing is that it is a process. A student will not receive perfect scores on their papers throughout the school year. Parents must look at the progress made from month to month, read the teacher's remarks, and celebrate the good parts that they wrote.

Too many parents are concerned about their child's grades. Some schools use the letter grade A-F and some use a rubric letter system from B-E (Beginning, Developing, Secure, and Exceeds). No matter what grading is used, it is important to celebrate your child's grade no matter what level.

When a student is in the elementary level, parents need to realize that this is the level where students learn how to follow directions and read to learn. They can later apply previous assignments to what they just learned to create higher level work. When there is a consistent push for your child to always make an A or secure grade, actual learning is lost. They are only concerned with the grade and not the subject or the knowledge.

In some districts, parents can become very competitive when it comes to their kid's grades and accomplishments. At this moment, you can either take charge or fall into that trap. It should not be a contest and letting them know you are not playing that game the better.

Remember, every district has its own show offs and competitive parents. Realize that it isn't important that your child get 100% on every assignment because of you doing their work. Your child getting their grades based on their own merit is how to play the game. Letting your children and the other parents know your opinion creates a calmer household for you and a possible lesson to others.

Writing Tips Now for Future College Essays

As they practice different types of writing, they will learn new styles, vocabulary, and transitions to use to advance their writing skills. If a student has a low grade throughout the year, use the conference meetings that are held two or three times a year to ask questions.

Some questions to ask can be what areas in writing are they doing well and what areas do they need improvement. Gather info you can use at home to help them, and share your concerns with the teacher. Teachers have many writing sites for parents to use to help them understand the writing process, so they can help their child.

Remember, anything your child learns at school will reflect the same journey they took when they learned to roll over, crawl, walk, hold a bottle, and hold a spoon and Sippy cup. We allowed them to practice over and over as we gave our full support. We encouraged, offered congratulations on what they learned successfully, and showed our love for their victories.

In the same way, we must support their learning in school. If keeping them motivated is the problem, use rewards and consequences that suit them and the work. For example, if there is an upcoming event that they want to attend, remind them that by performing at their best level and putting effort into their writing, they will be able to attend the function. If they do not put forth a higher level of work, it is up to the parent to use the consequence and not allow them to attend.

Once children do not get what they want, they will realize that you mean business. After they miss an event, offer another reward to get them back on track. They will begin to see how the world works. When you do the right thing, good things come to you. When you don't do what's right, you will have to overcome your negative choice.

They may want a new version of a computer game coming out soon or want to attend a school dance. Remind them to take a risk and try their best. Doing this also shows them you are monitoring their work. Let them realize that they don't have to be Stephen King, but they do have to take a risk and try writing down what comes into their head. Using your household modem works also. By clicking off the connection to internet, a child may feel motivated to complete their work.

When you pass along the fact that as they try, they move up the grade level, they will learn that an A or S for secure is not important to receive right away. It is in fact the end goal for the end of the year. If you want a positive attitude on both ends, only use positive thoughts and words. These create the outcome you want.

Chapter 14

The Scholar Athlete in all Her Glory

"What makes you comfortable can ruin you, and what makes you uncomfortable is the only way to grow."

~Bill Eckstrom

Whatever happens in their world, these successful scholar athletes are aware that it is easier to let things happen rather than make them happen. That doesn't mean they don't show up or fill out the necessary paperwork. They do what is necessary on their end and have a deep knowing that the rest is in sight. In addition, they have a tendency to act spontaneously rather than from fears based on past experiences. They do not let anything or anyone get in their way. Most importantly, they do not wallow in the recreation of judging themselves.

Furthermore, they are usually children who have been raised with my four keys of schedule, communication, consistency, and most importantly love. They are usually the ones who listened to their parents and wave to their moms in the stands yelling thanks.

Balance It All

When scholar athlete is mentioned, I believe that it does not strictly mean a sport, but any kind of art. It can include someone staying focused in their sport, any type of painting, music, debate, and writing. The word scholar remains the same throughout all types of art. These souls are already living their lives by their wants and follow their dreams. They are the children who do not have parents getting in the way of their dreams.

These strong minds have learned to have a balance in all things necessary to be prosperous. From healthy eating to healthy resting, scholar athletes or scholar artists know the secret to selecting and maintaining aspects from their lives to excel. They are connected with their families and friends, hard working, fearless, and know how and when to have fun.

Within these important aspects for success, these individuals use the four keys of consistency, communication, schedule, and love. Successful students follow their own heart which in turn helps them remain in bliss. There is a point in the lives of successful students where they are aware that they cannot attend every activity.

There were many a time when my daughters gave up a fun party or football game because studying for an exam was more important to them. Because some teachers in high school offered six o'clock early morning study sessions, they would complete their work and hit their bed early in order to get enough rest for the early morning study time. It was part of their success that they understood and were able to give up some things for others. It was this preconceived perception that helped them stay excited and focused on their path.

Get Out of Their Way

If I demanded that my eldest stay a volleyball player instead of staying with her love of swimming, she would have never been recognized for her achievements and merits in that sport. Because her parents were willing to go on her journey with her as the guide, she was able to execute and perform what was necessary for her to progress toward her dream.

Parents must remember that their child's life isn't theirs. Parents need to realize that they are similar to the artist that molds the clay. As your child moves toward their dreams, we have to guide, help, and support. Keep in mind that as parents, we may not have reached our dreams but that's ok. We need to respect their choices and know that we can follow our dreams later.

When we let our children live their lives, we are actually helping our children possess leadership skills. By letting go of the control, parents are helping their children transform into ambitious leaders.

Overcoming Adversity

My youngest fell in love with volleyball after she watched her older sister play during middle school and freshman years. She met a gold medalist from the Olympics while she attended middle school. She went on to play for national teams and became the first recruit for her class in college. But at the age of twelve, she found herself on a team that was run by a player's parent. Her life would learn how complexity would actually help.

Because we always practiced listening to their frustrations, sitting in the pain with them, and being with them during the complexities in their lives, our daughters experienced how to deal with complexity.

The Concept of Complexity

A second quote that helps is from Bill Eckstrom who has a powerful Tedx Talk about how complexity can help your life. He states, "What makes you comfortable can ruin you, but only in a state of discomfort can you continually grow." I thought about it and connected it to parents and our struggle to help our children and not hinder them.

Parents' ultimate goal is making their child happy, always. Bottom line, we will do anything for them to avoid any frustration in their life. As they begin to walk and fall, we want to do it for them to keep them from the feeling of frustration. As they play at the park or learn to ride their bike, we want to limit any amount of pain and suffering they feel.

What if I told you that studies show keeping your child/student in a state of order or comfort will prevent him/her from growth? It is already known through studies, such as University of Rochester Medical Center, that the brain doesn't fully develop until the age of 25. Knowing this, parents should try to keep in mind that they are the guides of their child's mind and brain. Another study using applied science is Bill Eckstrom's concept of Complexity Rings that shows how discomfort from your ordered life can actually help you grow.

Eckstrom's concept of complexity can occur three ways: it can be forced on you, it can come from others, or it can come from yourself. An example of it forced on you can be a loss of a parent as a pre-teen or an adult losing their job. This complexity makes you live outside your comfort zone. Because we like to eat and live in a home, we immediately react to the complexity forced on us and move towards the things we need.

A second example of complexity comes from others such as a mentor, coach, or parent. This is where we, as parents and educators, come in. It's up to us to help guide our child through the complexity in a way where we can be available to help when they ask. We should not tell them how to accomplish any problem. They need to do it on their own. A great example is having your child do the majority of the paperwork, essays, and research when they are entering the college search. By having your child take control of the reigns, the maturity and growth begins to surface. Letting them step out of your shadow is a bit scary, however sit back, applaud, and watch them grow.

The third example is a way of creating the complexity on ourselves. By stepping into unchartered waters in order to begin a new career or new project, you are throwing yourself into the feeling of unfamiliar territory. It keeps us on our toes, it makes us think outside the box, and we look into other areas that we might not have looked earlier for fear of not feeling safe.

Order vs. Complexity

A life of order in every aspect at every minute has nothing but predictability. Within this predictability, we feel safe. Don't get me wrong, a child's life should have some order. That's what keeps them feeling happy and secure. However, parents need to be careful of how much order they are creating for their child.

Bill Eckstrom stated in his video, "The key to growing is living where there is a limited amount of predictability to avoid order. Letting them live in the complexity is actually the best thing we can do." We are their training wheels in their life. Sometimes we have to take the step and announce to them that the training wheels are coming off. Letting them know that we are near to help guide is important, but we also want to send the message that it's time for them to take off down the road on their own.

During an intermission between the volleyball matches one Saturday, my daughter told me she was quitting and sprinted to our van. In the van, she cried and told her frustrations as well as stated her complexity. She stated she was going to quit, it wasn't fair, and she wasn't going to put up with this type of behavior from someone else. As a parent, we immediately feel their pain and we want to take it away as soon as we possibly can. Yet, as parents who want to see our child grow, we must refrain.

Inside Complexity

After she let all her frustration out, we sat in the car. I let her sit in her feelings. Something inside me asked her if she wanted my opinion. She said yes, so I started asking her what she wanted. In the next few minutes of the conversation, we laid out her choices and let her mull them over. I didn't show any bias towards any one position. I knew this had to come from her.

At this point in her life, she was already involved in swimming and volleyball. In swimming, she was part of a gold medal relay team of girls in Junior Olympics. By presenting her with the choices of each sport, the pros and cons of each, and the way that complexity will make its way into her life, it was now her call and her time to take control.

It was the time to let her feel the complexity of not always playing in every match. Although her future goal was to play in college, she wasn't sure if this was what she wanted. As she thought, she voiced how much she loved the sport of volleyball over swimming even though she was already making a splash. In addition, she let on that she loved learning new strategies and plays. She was on her way becoming coachable thanks to me allowing her to stay in complexity.

The Magic of Complexity

This is where the magic happens, but parents need to see that they must let go of the control and let their child pick. Instead on taking control, the best thing to do is speak of a time when complexity came into your life and share it with your child. Telling the truth about the hard times you endured is crucial to your child in order to understand that this is a growth stage. Be sure to tell all the wonderful things you learned along the way that helped strengthen your soul and inner being.

Her mind was made up and she chose volleyball. She did turn out to be the number one recruit at Salve Regina University and was a starter as a freshman making it to their division playoffs winning. That's a great achievement after knowing what happened to her in our van that Saturday. Although she was injured in sophomore and junior years, she came back to play most of her senior year. Because of her growth, she was selected by her church to help coach volleyball in Hungary on their mission that summer.

Complexity is Growth

When complexity comes, we are nudged to leave the sweet spot of comfort and venture out into the unknown. It is vital to explain to your child that staying in a place of comfort is not going to help them move forward. It will only keep them in one place. Yes, when everything is in order and never changes, we know and can predict the outcome. However, leaving our child in this state of order only helps them feel safe for that short moment. Down the road, staying in predictability will help them in that short instance, but only keep them from their growth towards their success.

There is a funny commercial seen on TV which shows a grown man at a young age, about early 20's, being pushed around in the shopping cart at a grocery store by his mom. He is definitely in his comfort zone and his mom has let him hide there from any complexity. It is hilarious to watch, but how many parents are actually raising their children and letting them stay in the place of order?

Growth = Success

We have to remember to allow our children to feel the uncomfortable awkward feelings that go along with change. When we feel like we're falling apart, it's really the universe creating something big in our life. It only feels this way because we're uncomfortable. In actuality, this awkward feeling is the path towards our success. As we model this in our lives and live by this statement in front of our children, we become the mentors that we were called on to guide these children of ours.

Because my daughter was left in complexity with her sport, she emerged the ultimate winner. She learned to attack and take on the complex feelings, she was the one who chose her destiny, and at the end of her rainbow, she learned that all along she was put on this path to have a lasting effect on youngsters half way around the world. By sharing her adversity of standing on the sideline and injury, she showed other girls that they could attain their goals, too.

In the end, it is clear to see. Living in order all the time is predictable and has a great feeling that goes along with it. However, we will never realize our actual potential. It is by living in these moments of complexity where we find growth.

Be sure to have some order in your home to create peace and tranquility, yet be sure to venture into complexity when things are starting to feel easy and predictable. Remind yourself that the awkward feeling is pointing you in the right directions. Breathe as you see your child enter their complexity, and remember that it will help them grow to be their best.

Chapter 15
Price of Knowledge

"Knowledge is Power"

~Francis Bacon

College is an expensive endeavor. If your child is not interested in attending, it is wise to save your hard working money and let them venture into other areas. Because the cost of college can be significant, there are ways of getting the most from your high school.

When my daughters attended high school, they registered for as many AP or Advanced Placement courses as they could each year. Since they were students who enjoyed the challenge, they found themselves taking up to ten of these courses. When applying for colleges, this was a big plus and also saved them a large amount of money because they passed the AP exams in high school. This gave them the credits toward their private colleges they selected. After their first freshman semester, they were both taking sophomore level classes.

Because they had the capability and the willingness to work hard in high school, they both saved money and achieved greatly. Robert F. Kennedy once stated, "Only those who dare to fail greatly can ever achieve greatly." Both girls lived through adversity and got a taste of failure during their journeys, but they both went after their fears head on.

While they took the initiative to study at great lengths by taking on many AP classes, one daughter graduated a four year college with two majors and two minors, and the other daughter received her MBA in four and a half years vs. up to six. Children who are given the room to move at their pace and toward their interests become great students who will one day be great achievers.

Starting the College Process

As your scholar finishes their sophomore year in high school, it is wise to dip your toe into the world of college and the application process. Things are very different from the 80's and 90's when we picked a college on our own. With so much going on in our lives, best advice to all parents is to look into the process early.

Second best advice for parents is to let their child select their university based on the career and interests they have. The fact that a parent attended the university should not be the focus. Although, be aware that certain schools offer discounts if alumni children attend the same school, so be sure to look into all information. Honestly, you will save yourself from additional white hairs and stress by dipping into the college process.

The college process has many steps and can be a scary place. Acquaint yourself with the new vocabulary lingo, process, and important dates for certain forms. It is the time to search your bank statements and have a discussion with your accountant on the importance of finishing your taxes early and filling out important paperwork to help your student attend a school out of state.

By arming yourself with a college mentor, he will be able to walk you through the very extensive process and answer all questions big and small. These mentors may cost up to $1,500 but when your child is considering a $50,000 a year school, the money the mentor saves you through scholarships and grants is significant.

Matching the college to your child's needs, interests and career should be the task at hand. Questions about the size, location, weather, and professor-to-student ratio are among the main points to start your search. Nowadays, there are websites where you can input your high school transcripts along with your interests. My daughters used www.collegeboard.org.

Message to the Rising Senior

The remaining sections are written to the rising senior. My information is towards the one looking into a college. So as you read through the next few sections, remember that when I say you, I am talking to the college bound student.

By putting in the characteristics of what type of college wanted, it can provide you with the requirements for submissions. There are areas such as whether they take an SAT or ACT score, the essay topic, their due dates for early action or regular submission and much more. Consider how large of a population you want your future college to be as well as its location. If you don't mind snow and cold weather as part of your experience, look into schools on the east coast.

Remember, schools in your home state can only accept a certain percentage of residents. If you are from an area such as CA, the colleges, mainly UCs, only accept certain percentage of CA students. The rest will be selected from out-of-state. As a reminder, some people begin looking after finishing their sophomore year in high school. Heads up, the essay topics change every year for each college/university.

Furthermore, this website will also let you know which colleges will likely accept YOU. By putting in your GPA, sports skills, residence, theater abilities, community service, and outside hobbies, you will find out which universities and colleges will likely accept you before you begin their application and essays. This helps avoid wasting your time on schools that will most likely not accept you.

The Well-Rounded Individual

Keep in mind that colleges are not only looking at grades and possible sports abilities. They're looking for well-rounded individuals with involvement in community service. At a young age, we introduced our girls to community service at their local church and school. They helped serve lunches to the seniors and organize food banks at their church.

In addition, they offered their time at their elementary school when they were in middle school to read with other students and help them with their homework at an after school program. Be advised that some food banks and pet shelters have an age requirement. Think back to all your experiences and ask your parents for their memories of you serving others.

The Writing Process Begins

Once you have a list of about 8-10 schools that will accept you based on your grades, sports, arts, and outside experiences, now it's time to schedule writing essays each day.

There is the Common Application that all schools want to see, which might be the first essay to begin. Yes, as you read the different topics for each school, you will see that you can borrow paragraphs here and there from other essays you have been writing. Be sure to stick to the topics and use only paragraphs that give a full and complete answer. Using the same essay to fit another's topics is frowned upon.

As you begin scheduling these essays during your junior summer, you will see there is not much time for a lot of summer fun. This process is important, but so is your sanity. Be sure to schedule some pool or beach time with friends, but remember there will not be a lot of time at the beginning of senior year.

Schedule Time to be a Senior

There are many senior events and if you are an athlete, all your down time is consumed with staying on top of your studies.

Keep in mind that universities and colleges look at your senior year grades as well. They want to offer scholarships to those who will consistently make good grades, so be sure your grades aren't forfeited because you're bogged down with college essays at the beginning of your senior year.

Now that you are totally excited and have a bit of knowledge with some research of schools, start thinking about scheduling time to put together video clips of your sport, drama plays, and debates you have. Prepare the best selections and send those out to the athletic or theater directors of the schools you are most interested.

When put in the right hands, these videos can help you receive more scholarship. Because a Division I or II school pretty much owns their athletes, my girls selected Division III schools with their sports. They focused on the schools that were the best for their careers and fields of study. The coaches who see your amazing videos will go to their department heads and get your scholarship money. Yes, Division III schools don't give athletic scholarships, but the department heads will look at your scholar side of grades, extracurricular activities, and community service.

Since most schools will not honor your athletic scholarship if injured, be sure to cover yourself by having other options. By researching schools where you can get the best knowledge for your career, you will study at a university where you can spread your wings as an athlete as well as learn every important aspect for your future.

Take Action with Early Action

Sometime in November is usually the important date for those seeking early action. Early action is a way to apply to some colleges that are your favorites. (Not all schools offer early action.) This is usually done by students that have done extensive college research, have found a college(s) that strongly matches academically, socially, and geographically, meet and exceed in the SAT/ACT requirements, and has an academic record that has been consistently solid over time.

By applying at the early action dates, you benefit from admissions seeing your name early. You will remain on their mind before others who apply later in January/February. It is a way of putting your best foot forward and shows them you really want to attend their school. Since less people do early action, the admissions department spends more time looking at your application.

Questionnaire for Athletes

As a scholar athlete, be sure to fill out the school's sports questionnaire form. It will alert the athletic director and coaches of that college you are interested in playing with them. If this is done in July, this gives you a head start over others. My daughter filled this out and sent video to the head coach. The coach followed up with her by phone call, email and visited the business departments to help her receive scholarship. She received 90% of their tuition every year because of her volleyball skills, but mostly for her high grades.

Venturing Elsewhere Pays Off

Not everyone wants to go far from home when attending college, but it you don't mind and want to live in different seasons, be sure to look at colleges across the country. Both of my CA daughters found private liberal arts schools on the east coast. Because they knew they would only be there for four years, they picked schools with amazing foliage and snow days. They were lucky to have family friends and some family on the east coast.

Although they didn't fly home for Thanksgiving, they have made it home for every Christmas and summer. We adjusted to spending Thanksgiving differently with our college girls by finding different friends and family to share the holiday. The most important thing about finding a school on the east coast is they offer more scholarship to students from the west coast in order to be more diverse.

Enjoy the Process

After reading this your head is probably ready to explode. It is a lot of information to take in so reread it a few times. As you begin the college process, begin to make notes on a calendar, make to-do lists, and schedule your essay writing days. Most of all make your parents aware of the dates to get important forms filed.

There may be college consultants in your area, so take time to seek them out. Even though this seems difficult and intricate, take your time. Include your parents, family members, and even your high school teachers. Think about emailing your essays to your English teachers, they will be happy to help. It is customary to send a cover letter asking for their time to read and critique your writing and be sure to say thank you with a card and small token.

It sounds like your summer will be spent writing the majority of your days, so stock up your fridge with your favorite snacks, microwavable meals, and healthy summer fruits. As you begin finishing the research, applications and essays, you will notice how much time it all takes. You will be so grateful your mom found this chapter to help you get ready.

Remember, you're a senior and it's time to start acting like one. Take responsibility for your future. Don't think you have lots of time; you really don't. Dive into your pool for a quick dip and then hit the laptop! Get moving on selecting your future college, you will not regret it.

Most of all enjoy the process. Every time you feel you've hit a wall, talk it out with your parents, siblings, or friends. Remember, it is only fear creeping in and trying to scare you. Keep a smile on your face, put as much time and effort into the process, and have fun. Good luck on your future endeavors. It will work out the way you want it!

Chapter 16

The Circle is Complete

"Give the ones you love wings to fly, roots to come back, and reasons to stay."

~The Dalai Lama

For those of you who like to skip to the end, believe me, it all turns out fine. All the hard work you put in pays off. By using the four keys of scheduling, consistency, communication, and especially love throughout the raising of your scholar athletes, you end up with independent and loving children living as responsible adults.

No Magic Pill

As you can see, there is no magic word, phrase, pill, or strategy that can be used once to guide your angel to greatness. However, by raising them using my four keys and strategies, I have received such wonderful kindnesses back. They know how to go out into the world and seek their passion. They know how to take charge of their own lives and find jobs or employment to help them on their way. Your children who become scholar athletes take ownership of their life by paying their own bills and taking on their own insurance. It truly is an amazing sight.

Both of my children had to find jobs once their scholarships ran out in order to stay across country and finish their education to the level that they wanted. They had to learn how to live within their means and live through the struggle of getting by. They had to learn how to rely on and motivate themselves by walking into the real world using positive self talk.

Set Love as the Rule

My belief is that avoiding shame within our household was the number one thing that started the ball rolling for my girls becoming the scholar athletes they wanted to be. Once this rule is set and followed through, the other strategies fall into place. Don't get me wrong, raising children this way doesn't promise them to become successful at college, it does, however, set them up with the important life skill of keeping consistent.

Since I lived as a child in a house that didn't encompass love, I knew that was the ingredient that I needed to add to my own life. I made sure my children knew how much I loved them by taking the time to go through the grounding consequences. Ultimately, my eldest sent me a text as her swim team in college was traveling back to their university. She witnessed the outcome of an individual who always received what she wanted. This swimmer threw a total and childish fit because the slice of pizza that she received had a burnt bubble on it. My text literally thanked me for not raising her to be an unfeeling jerk. She gave me thanks for holding her accountable for her actions so she didn't turn out like the donkey that was acting up in front of her.

The Intangible Gifts

I have to say, that is the best acknowledgement of success for me. This eldest daughter who is an archaeologist had a t-shirt made for her team in Cyprus during one of her digs that said, "Pilar didn't raise a bitch!" Dang, I have to admit, that was kind of the icing on the cake. When they put it in writing, you know they understand.

Among our fears, dilemmas, and missteps are the life lessons for us to learn. In your difficult parenting situations, always look for the lesson that you are to learn along with your child. Remember, our child is here to help us learn the lessons we haven't learned yet.

As a parent, we sometimes end up in a space where we feel we cannot get out. The event will feel so hard, hopeless, continuous, and overwhelming that we fear it will never end. That is the time when we have to use our faith and respond in an opened manner. Pull faith out and sit with it. Take time to slow yourself and live in that very minute. Look at the circumstances and smile, because you are about to learn your lesson.

Lessons Learned

As my daughters had a meltdown over a failing grade and dealt with the bruised femur, they taught me to practice doing only what I could manage. I was taught to practice taking account of my actions as I move through my journey. I learned, at that moment, to only include those things that will bring me joy and help me meander through my tour of life.

As you twist and turn through this time as a parent, remain close to the idea that everything your child needs to learn will show up. When these lessons appear, be open to learn from their test because more likely it is something you need as well.

During these parenting moments, it is important to keep in mind on a constant basis that our children act out when they are hurting. It can be anywhere from a small hurt of someone calling them a name to a constant feeling of loneliness. They may not feel adequate, or they may not feel that they are enough in some way. As a parent, it is our job to help them learn how to get themselves from that point of unhappiness to the point where they feel confident to move onward on their own feet. This will elevate them to becoming the scholar athlete they've always wanted.

Complexity Makes Them Grow

As parents, we want to wish away all their pain and all their tears. We want them to live in constant joy and happiness. Little do we know that if we continue to create the happiness for them, they will never learn the skills they need on their own. They need to learn to stand on their own two feet without leaning on anyone. Even through all the circumstances that are not positive, they need to learn to lean on themselves. By listening to Bill Eckstrom's Tedx Talk and recalling his quotes, remember that when your child is uncomfortable, they are actually growing. This uncomfortable feeling is for them to experience and move through.

Thinking of Michael Bernard Beckwith's words about our purpose, he states, "Our human purpose here on earth is to unfold our soul." We are not all here to be millionaires, super rich, or famous. We are, however, here to do that which is instructed by God in order to help others. If our passion and joy comes from writing, our words are there to help others out of their pain and back on their journey. That is God's will for us.

Practice Makes Purpose

We are all here to fulfill our purpose. Our purpose is in some way a service to another. As a parent, our child's journey is predicated on the knowledge that we guide, nurture, and teach them how to reach inward and learn how to hold onto the Divine that is within all of us.

Being a parent is the best lesson of all. As I watch my girls venture off into their lives, I am in awe of their tenacity and how far they have gone on their journey already. I see how faith, guidance, opening up to them, sharing my feelings, and using oneness has transformed them to take all their lessons and begin to travel down their life's road and purpose. I truly see how my four keys of Love, Schedule, Communication, and Consistency helped me guide them towards what they needed to learn as well as demonstrate to me the lessons I needed to learn or revise.

They have moved on toward their dreams and purpose. As they both ventured off to the east coast to study, they learned all the things they're passionate about. One daughter ventured off to the Middle East many times to work with other archaeologists at her graduate university to practice cataloging his findings and do some digging herself. My other daughter went off to Spain in her junior semester using her second language for her travel abroad experience.

When you are watching your children in those hard times, remind them they are not alone, seek the lesson for yourself, reach out to others that can help in the community of friends, family, and schools, and practice staying in oneness. God is always offering up his guidance and answers. We have to be opened to receive it. Stay in that place of harmony.

Conquer Your Fear

One important attribute a successful scholar overcomes is fear. "Never, never, never give up", were the inspirational words from Winston Churchill. In order to be successful, one has to fail in order to learn from their mistake. Scholar athletes thrive in the word 'try'. Successful people will try everything they can to meet their goal. If that means failure will occur, they are willing to go through the process. They continuously work toward their dream no matter the circumstances. They look at it as the more they fail, the more they learn, and succeed.

In all honesty, my youngest who was a valuable volleyball player in college only made her high school team as a freshman. Since the volleyball program was very intricate, it was hard to be chosen. Each tryout from sophomore year to senior year always ended with her being the last to be cut. As these disappointments happened, it only helped her strategize ways to try again and never giving up even when a goal wasn't achieved.

If they did not have the setbacks and lessons along their adolescent years, and if we gave them everything they wanted, they would be here at home taking advantage. They would have never learned how to live on their own, or learned how to go about finding their own housing and roommates. The world would have swallowed them up and spit them out on our couch. They would not be reaching toward their dreams.

I see all the hard work come full circle. So as a parent who has gone into those fearful places with her children, I can attest to you there is light at the end of the tunnel. They do learn the lessons that they need and they do move on toward their purpose. Letting go of my ego, accepting my own mistakes, sharing my love, and acknowledging the turmoil as the life lessons sent by God, I see how those lessons and hard work help create the unfolding of another's beautiful path.

Angels Unawares

When my eldest was a three year old, she noticed a group of trees that were by the side of a highway in our town. One day she suggested we get ice cream cones and go sit and eat them under the trees. Because she mentioned it several times, I decided to do it for two reasons. First, there was always a homeless person sitting there. I wanted her to know that there are all types of people in the world no matter where she wanted to venture off. As we pulled over and parked, she got out and sat near the man. She wasn't bothered by him but rather enjoyed his company.

Secondly, I remember how she wasn't afraid to tell him she always wanted to eat her ice cream in this place. She followed through and did what she wanted. I recall the smile that came to his face. It reminded me of the scripture in Hebrews where we shouldn't forget to show hospitality to strangers, for some who have done this have entertained angels without realizing it. My inclination is that she knew.

The same thing happened in the park in NYC when she was a bit older. We were on the hunt to find Balto's statute. She saw a man who looked like he needed some food so she asked me for some money to give to him. After I gave her a $5 bill, she and her sister ran off to give it to him. Their aunt, my best friend, reminded me of that saying, "Some have entertained angels unawares." This friend always noticed how her nieces, my daughters, were always seeking out these angels. These moments helped my daughters practice doing what they wanted without having fear. I didn't put my worry or fear of the moment on them.

Although technology can be addicting, I'm grateful for it. If it wasn't for the ability to FaceTime, make a quick call, or simply text a quick hello, I don't know how I would have fared. We were able to watch their steamed swim meets and volleyball games. Being on the other coast was hard, but having these options made the distance tolerable. Seeing the fun and goofy Snapchats as they traveled to their sporting events always put smiles on our faces as parents. We engaged in their fun and saw they were safe.

The Keys Unlock their Essence

As you can see, my four keys of consistency, communication, scheduling and love are the way into their hearts and minds. By being consistent with them, keeping the lines open with communication, and helping them to set up their schedules that will help them function, love is the overall key that covers them all. They all need love in order for them to work.

If you look at it, love is the ingredient for it to all work well. As we move through a recipe, if we are missing an important ingredient, the cake comes out crumby. However, if you follow the recipe step by step and do all the necessary things needed, it comes out beautiful.

The best feeling in the world as a parent is seeing your children as grown adults living in the world and following their passion toward their purpose. Watching them showing and sharing their love with others they have met along the way is priceless. Knowing that they were able to overcome their fears is stunning. Seeing how God has put so many wonderful people along their path to help them along their journey is the most precious gift to receive as a parent.

A Job Well Done

In that, I know in my heart that I graduated as a parent. I learned what I was supposed to learn from them. I see how all those long hours of advising, discussing, and wrestling with thoughts of bad and good had their place in my own lessons. Now, they are giving back to us.

One November, we found a secondhand car when our other car died. We borrowed the money from the eldest until payday. She turned around and said Merry Christmas. The following fall, she flew us to a family friend's wedding back east. We bought the hotel rooms and meals. It is the best feeling in the world to see your children acting like true caring individuals.

Churchill stated, "Success is going from failure to failure with great enthusiasm." Parents that stay out of the way of their children's dreams will one day sit at their child's college graduation in awe of all their accomplishments.

As you sit watching your youngsters learn to crawl, try out for sports, and travel the world, spread your joy and love all around your environment. You will feel it circle back tenfold. Be ready to go after your own passions when your children leave home to find theirs. It comes up very quickly, but it is the best surprise when it shows up. You realize that you have so much to offer. Look into what gives you joy and fuels your passion. Take the steps to nurture yourself now that you've nurtured your angels. Collect all the wisdom you learned and venture off to spread your own wings. Pat yourself on the back. You did good!

Bibliography

"What Sleep Is and Why All Kids Need It." *KidsHealth - the Web's Most Visited Site about Children's Health*. The Nemours Foundation, n.d. Web. 25 May 2016.

"Children and Sleep." *Children & Sleep*. National Sleep Foundation, n.d. Web. 25 May 2016.

"Cry It out." *TODAY.com*. N.p., n.d. Web. 29 May 2016.

Lauren Hale Ph.d. National Sleep Foundation video

"Why Screen Time before Bed Is Bad for Children." *The Conversation*. N.p., n.d. Web. 11 June 2016.

"Viewing ADHD Differently." *Your Treatment Guide for ADHD (Attention Deficit Hyperactivity Disorder)*. ADD Referral, 28 June 2012. Web. 19 July 2016.

J.S. Shonkoff & D. Phillips, Eds., *From Neurons to Neighborhoods: The Science of Early Childhood Development (2000), Washington D.C.; National Research Council & The Institute of Medicine, National Academy Press*.

"An Interview with Daniel Goleman." *American Scientist*. The Sigma Xi, The Scientific Research Society, 2016. Web. 10 July 2016.

"Social-Emotional Learning, Why It Matters." *Cfchildren.org*. Committee for Children, 2016. Web. 10 July 2016.

Goleman, Daniel. "Emotional Intelligence - Daniel Goleman." *Daniel Goleman*. N.p., n.d. Web. 10 July 2016.

the Bible, Proverbs 16:24 NLT

"What It Takes to Be a Fully Present Parent - SuperSoul.tv." *SuperSoultv*. N.p., 15 May

Parent: Transforming Ourselves, Empowering Our Children. Vancouver: Namaste Pub., 2010. Print.

Kahn, Matthew. *Whatever arises Love that*. Boulder: Sounds True, Inc., 2016. Print.

Achor, Shawn. The Happiness Advantage: The Seven Principals of Psychology That Fuel Success and Performance at Work. New York: Crown Business, 2010. Print

Dyer, Wayne. *Living The Wisdom of The Tao*. Carlsbad: Hayhouse, 2007. Print

Http://www.youtube.com/channel/UCHgM01h7sVA8AoeF8JivbfQ. "Living The Wisdom Of The Tao - Dr Wayne Dyer." *YouTube*. YouTube, 10 Feb. 2015. Web. 08 Oct. 2016.

"Elizabeth Lesser (Full Episode) - SuperSoul.tv." *SuperSoultv*. N.p., 30 Sept. 2016. Web. 09 Oct. 2016.

*Add Common Sense Media Source for Technology chapter

Taylor, Jim. "How Technology Is Changing the Way Children Think and Focus." *Psychology Today*, Sussex Publishers, 4 Dec. 2012, www.psychologytoday. com/blog/the-power-prime/201212/how-technology-is-changing-the-way-children-think-and-focus.

Brennan, Dan. "2 Year Old Child Developmental Milestones." *WebMD*, WebMD, 29 Mar. 2019, www.webmd.com/parenting/guide/child-at-2-milestones#3.

Walters, Joanna. "Tablets and Smartphones May Affect Social and Emotional Development, Scientists Speculate." *The Guardian*, Guardian News and Media, 2 Feb. 2015, www.theguardian.com/technology/2015/feb/01/toddler-brains-research-smartphones-damage-social-development.

Talks, TEDx. "TEDxRainier – Dimitri Christakis – Media and Children." *YouTube*, YouTube, 28 Dec.2011, www.youtube.com/watch?v=BoT7qH_uVNo.

Eckstrom, Bill. "Why Comfort Will Ruin Your Life: Bill Eckstrom: TEDxUniversityofNevada." *YouTube*, 31 Jan. 2017, youtu.be/LBvHI1awWaI.

About the Author

Pilar was a stay-at-home mom before stepping into her teaching phase. She has over eighteen years experience in education as a credentialed teacher, a reading teacher, and resource teacher in special education. As she perfected her skills in teaching, she was able to help use her important keys to help produce two scholar athletes; her daughters. By helping to guide her daughters in the scholar athlete world, one was the first volleyball selection for Salve Regina University earning an MBA, and another daughter swam for Lycoming College receiving two degrees in Archaeology & Art History while finishing her PhD at Temple University. Pilar's strengths lie in her ability to reach children and let them recognize their own strengths. Her next book will help parents in the empty nest stage. She lives in Encinitas, CA with her husband and daughters' cats enjoying the beach, writing, and fishing.

Made in the USA
Middletown, DE
14 September 2021

48308469R00119